"*Power Beliefs* deftly explains how we program our destiny through a strategic chess match played out within each of our individual belief systems. Author Steven E. Carr reveals the categories, the hierarchies, and ultimately a workbook-style strategy by which we can reprogram the subconscious mind for maximum success."

~ **Jack Canfield**, Co-Author *Chicken Soup For The Soul* series, motivational speaker, corporate trainer.

POWER BELIEFS

THE SECRET TO UNLOCKING
YOUR DREAMS MAY BE
ONE BELIEF AWAY

Steven E. Carr

m

Ashtin McKrey Publishing
Columbus, Ohio

STAY INSPIRED.
The world depends upon it.

Acknowledgments

Jami S. Oliver - you are perched at the utmost apex of my acknowledgments for the inspiration, patience, collaboration, and advice you provided for this book to manifest. I love you. Thank you for cheerfully walking alongside me during this effort.

I cannot thank enough those who spent their precious time to beta-read this book and provide me with so much valuable advice and feedback. Thank you, thank you!

Cassandra Burghdorf, Michael Carrier, Dan Cook, Rick Crossland, Kathryn R. Gugle, Ashley Hill, Scott Rabin, Scott Seeley, and Kimba Wawrzyniak. This book is far better because of your inputs.

Printed in the United States of America

First Printing, 2020

ISBN: 978-1-7359920-0-6 (paperback)
ISBN: 978-1-7359920-1-3 (eBook)

Ordering Information:

Quantity sales. Special discounts are available on quantity purchases by corporations, associations, and others. For details, contact the publisher at the website: StevenECarr.com.

Contents

Introduction 1

SECTION I:
Power Beliefs: What Are They?........................5

Chapter 1: The Loophole 7

Chapter 2: Viktor, George, & Roger 13

SECTION II:
The Categories, Rules, & Strategy Of The Game...........21

Chapter 3: Mental Feng Shui................................23

Chapter 4: Belief Assessment..............................29

Chapter 5: A Belief = ...35

Chapter 6: The Detroit Lions Vs. The Sunrise..................37

Chapter 7: How Your Mind Categorizes Beliefs.............43

Chapter 8: Alphas..47

Chapter 9: Truths..51

Chapter 10: Facts..55

Chapter 11: Values...59

Chapter 12: Opinions.......................................65

Chapter 13: Superstitions 71

Chapter 14: Hopes..75

SECTION III:
Where Do Beliefs Come From And Why? 79

Chapter 15: Origins Of Your Beliefs........................81

Chapter 16: Repetition.....................................91

Chapter 17: Compare And Contrast...........................95

Chapter 18: Emotion..99

Contents

SECTION IV:

The Purpose, Strengths, and Weaknesses Of Power Beliefs 103

Chapter 19: The Pablo Escobar Strategy...........................105

Chapter 20: Never Surrender...109

Chapter 21: The Force Field...115

Chapter 22: Warping Reality..121

Chapter 23: The Cool Clique..127

Chapter 24: Couples Therapy...131

SECTION V:

How To Reprogram Your Belief System.......................135

Chapter 25: The Scales Of Reality.....................................137

Chapter 26: STEP 1...145

Chapter 27: STEP 2...151

Chapter 28: STEP 3...157

Chapter 29: STEP 4...171

Chapter 30: STEP 5...181

Chapter 31: STEP 6...197

Chapter 32: STEP 7...201

BELIEF ASSESSMENT REDO.......................................207

POWER BELIEFS

INTRODUCTION

I believe each and every human lives and dies with un-tapped potential. And I literally mean every human: even those we collectively deem as super-successful, even *they* have room to improve. Unfortunately, the great majority of us will die with so much more of *what could have been* trapped inside us. Our greatness, our dreams, our unique brilliance, these will not be fulfilled during our brief time on Earth.

Stop and consider that for a moment. Consider how many people (possibly yourself) will live, then die, and never experience the life they truly wanted. Is there any collective aspect of humanity as sad as that? Death is sad, of course, but the fact that nearly all of us will die having not lived the life we wanted, makes dying even more tragic.

Currently, there are about 7 billion humans on our planet playing out sad storylines which involve under-employment, loneliness, sickness, ignorance, poverty, defeat, failure, and unhappiness. Why? Does it need to be this way? Is there some Universal Law that says we can't all self-actuate? Why are so many of us stuck or stunted? One reason may be our tendency to identify both our problems and solutions with external factors. We assign blame to the external world; competition, discrimination, racism, bad parents, poor education, the economy, politics, greed, nepotism—the list is long. And if those culprits aren't formidable enough, we've gone

1

ahead and created an invisible force called *Bad Luck*, which is like sealing caulk, easily filling any blame gaps for which the other categories can't take credit. In the end, we start to believe our dreams are somehow being foiled by the seven billion other stories swimming alongside us, or by God, or fate...so we reluctantly, and gradually give up.

But giving up, which signals the end to our dreams, is not an external cause. Giving up is an internal decision. So maybe it's time we shift focus and deliberately seek solutions within the world of our minds where both our dreams and their surrender were created in the first place.

Recommending an introspective approach is, of course, an ancient prescription still preached by modern psychology, with the self-help pundits and motivational gurus all echoing the same advice:

- *Get rid of your limiting beliefs.*
- *Believe you can do it.*
- *Adopt empowering beliefs.*
- *If you believe it, you'll achieve it.*
- *Change your beliefs and you'll change your destiny.*

But, as of yet, they've never explained HOW! They promised that optimizing our beliefs would elevate our mindset and deliver our goals and yet, outside pumping us up with motivational hip-hip-hooray, we never got the blueprint on how to do it! Decades of self-help books, personal development seminars, and power retreats sold the same thing: an invisible treasure map with personalized vision boards and mantras acting as our only compass. I'm not suggesting the gurus were unscrupulous—merely ignorant themselves of how to navigate and execute the most critical requirement: **belief modification.**

To be fair, two excellent techniques geared toward reprogramming our beliefs are hypnosis and Neurolinguistic Programming (NLP). Both strategies are popularly misunderstood and are therefore, unfortunately and unfairly, mired in quasi-Occultism. Even though they are effective methodologies, they are avoided for either philosophical concerns or sheer skepticism.

This book offers a new approach for the 7 billion unfulfilled storylines trying to realize life's potential before the ticking clock stops. This book explains HOW to change your belief system. How to free yourself from limiting beliefs. How to reprogram your mind to serve your goals and dreams.

As a hypnotherapist with a background in communication-psychology, over 25 years experience in marketing and sales psychology, as well as NLP training, I've attempted to remove all the *woo-hoo* from understanding how our subconscious beliefs actually work.

Think of your belief system like software code. Software glitches are keeping you from your dreams and happiness. If we reprogram the mental code, we can eliminate the glitches. If we update your mental apps, we can open new doors to your future.

This is not mental magic—it's mental engineering. It's applied belief strategy. It's time to unleash your brilliance and I'm going to explain HOW. Together we'll unlock the mental chains keeping you from living the life of your dreams.

And the best news is—you may be only ONE belief away from anything you desire. Removing one limiting belief can initiate a domino effect that topples dozens of other limiting beliefs. Embedding one proactive Power Belief can activate a chain-reaction of positive transformation throughout your entire belief system.

On your death bed, it will not be the things you did while alive—all the mistakes and failures—that you'll regret. Instead it'll be the things you *didn't* do. The things you didn't try. The opportunities you didn't take. The dreams you let slip away. These will be the crushing regrets of your life.

But your clock is still ticking. Your life is still unfolding. My goal is to provide information to help you tap into your mind and unleash your highest abilities. Achieve your highest potentials. Live your best life possible.

The gurus were right—the solutions have always been inside you. Hiding within your belief system. It's time to shine light on that belief system. It's time to explore that invisible map.

POWER BELIEFS

WHAT ARE THEY?

Beliefs are choices. First you choose your beliefs.
Then your beliefs affect your choices.

~ Roy T. Bennett

CHAPTER 1

THE LOOPHOLE

Saturday May 21, 2011 was the worst day of my life. I was a 43-year-old father of four, living alone in a $650/month, tiny two-bedroom apartment in Columbus, Ohio. My marriage ended six months earlier and for the first time my kids were no longer a part of my daily life. I had no other family or friends in the entire state, and I had lost a great new job a few weeks earlier when the company that hired me got fired by the company that was outsourcing them. Financially, I was broke, and before the day ended, I would bankrupt both emotionally and spiritually.

If I had to choose two symbols to represent that day, the first would be a couch. The second a picnic table.

The couch rested along the outer wall of my living room, facing the tiny bachelor-sized kitchen. My apartment was on the second floor, and the main entrance was through that kitchen. I can't recall how long I sat alone on that green couch, staring a hundred miles into the distance...sitting motionless and silent. Breathing, and blinking...but otherwise paralyzed.

At some point my trance was broken by familiar sounds. I heard muffled giggles and the scurrying of feet up the fire-escape steps. It was my youngest two children, finally arriving for their weekend with Dad.

Earlier that morning I had visited my ex to pick up my kids. It was, after all, my weekend. Their mother, however, had invited them on some fun outing she and her new boyfriend had planned. She let the kids decide whether they would prefer going with her to the fun, outdoor, kid-friendly adventure or go back to dad's gloomy apartment. It was another loss for me, receiving zero votes. But she agreed to drop them off later.

I still remember the feeling coursing through me as I sat motionless on that couch, listening to my children knock on that door over and over and over again, and then call out to their mother below that I must not be home. And I remember the sound of their little feet descending the stairs, then fading away...the sound of a car door closing, the minivan pulling away...as I chose to let them go.

Late in the afternoon, I got up from the couch, left the apartment and began walking nowhere in particular. It quickly became clear that I should die. The absolute clarity and certainty of this decision startled me enough to question it. *Did I really want to die?* Maybe I was just being dramatic and feeling sorry for myself? To test my resolve, I imagined my children and all the milestones of their lives I would miss were I to die that day:

I would never see my son play high school sports. I didn't care.

I would never walk my younger daughters down the wedding aisle. I didn't care.

I would be absent from all their graduations and never meet any future grandchildren. Ever!

I can honestly say, none of those events triggered even the faintest emotional impact in my heart or soul. Oddly, my reasons to live all boiled down to the value I ascribed to just a handful of future memories. Living would only be to experience those milestones and I didn't care about those moments anymore. I wanted to die.

I had reached a moment of complete apathy towards everything I had once deemed significant. My children were the greatest joys of my life but the decision to never see them again was somehow as easy as hanging up on a telemarketer. I was both numb and empty to life.

There was one little hiccup, however—one wrinkle disrupting my newfound suicide plan, and it only appeared once I had decided to go forth. I had known two women whose fathers had committed suicide. I had glimpsed the turmoil and damage those deaths foisted upon their daughters' psyches and so I had decided long ago, I would never do that to my own children. Somehow, in my current belief system, it was acceptable to commit suicide, permissible to abandon my children at their young ages, but it was unacceptable to torment them further with the stigma of a suicide and so many unanswerable questions. To kill myself was okay—to hurt them, was not. But perhaps...maybe if a car jumped the curb and struck me dead...or if there was some other way to die without it appearing as suicide...yes, that would solve everything! It would of course, still hurt my children to have me die, but it would release them from knowing I did it on purpose.

I had to find a loophole; a way to have my cake and eat it too. And I knew I was smart enough to find one.

As I walked on, I came upon the second symbol of the day, an abandoned picnic table near a rarely used soccer field. Alone, I sat there thinking till it grew dark. I was giving my mind analytic overtime to come up with an answer on how to die without technically killing myself. There could be no obvious link between my death and any intent on my part. It had to appear like an accident and convince even the most seasoned investigators. It was a fascinating problem to solve. Since no one knew I was suicidal, they'd have no reason to suspect suicide. All I needed to do was figure out a way to guarantee reasonable doubt.

It does not surprise me that I eventually found a loophole. Our minds are programmed to solve problems. I eventually found a viable scenario to make everything work. What was it? I think toxic asphyxiation—but I honestly can't remember, because immediately upon finding a solution to the problem I was *released*—now free to glimpse the madness of the mission itself. Upon finding the loophole, my mind was released of its previous deep focus. It was no longer tethered to thoughts of how badly I wanted to die, nor to a crafty plot to disguise my suicide. I was temporarily free to think ANYTHING—and what rushed in to fill the vacuum was an understanding of how corrupted my thinking had become. How my mind had been operating on its own within a self-distorted loop. In this understanding, in having experienced my distorted thoughts as real and truthful, so many other corrupted minds instantly became understandable. I understood how all minds could bend and break given infected programming. I could fully relate to how mothers could intentionally drive their children into rivers. I understood murder, suicide, and all other tragic acts of desperation. So many of those whom we consider *monsters* or *lost souls* definitely did not see what was happening to them as they worked out their terrible solutions. I saw how we, ourselves, could cast the very spell that imprisons our mind and ruins us. Distorted programming creates a focus that steers us away from the red lights and flashing warning signs. In those brief moments after discovering the loophole, so much clarity came rushing to my awareness.

But why was I alive when others were not? Why had I not completely derailed? What differentiated me from other suicides?

It's my conclusion that my life was saved by a Power Belief—a dominant belief that completely controlled my thoughts and actions. My saving Power Belief was simply: suicide will destroy my children's future happiness.

That one belief bought me time. It put up a roadblock to suicide that forced me to find a work-around. The pain I was drowning in was suddenly put on the back burner so I could use my analytical left brain and find a loophole. In marshalling the deep focus needed to solve that complex, analytical problem, less energy was given to my emotional right brain. That delay—the span of an hour or two, gave me the distance and mental exhaustion needed to detach from my suicidal delusion. Relying so heavily on logic and calculation to find the loophole, once it was discovered, I could no longer relate to the emotional being who wanted to die. My life today is owed to a single belief that gave me time and distance. Gave me lots of time, in fact.

I hope in telling this story, I'm not falsely conveying that I understood Power Beliefs back at that picnic table. In the years following, becoming a hypnotherapist has provided me ample time to study and contemplate the strange workings of our minds. Gaining insight into Power Beliefs, it has now become my mission to help others understand the tremendous influence they hold over our lives; both the good and bad.

Control your Power Beliefs and you control your destiny.

CHAPTER 2

VIKTOR, GEORGE, & ROGER

It may be useful to introduce (or possibly reintroduce) three amazing true stories that all exemplify the Power Belief phenomena.

VIKTOR

The first takes place in Poland 1944, where an Austrian psychiatrist named Viktor Frankl finds himself imprisoned in the Nazi concentration camp of Auschwitz.

The Germans have pretty much destroyed everything that is precious to Viktor. They've stripped him of his career, his possessions, his freedom. They've killed his wife and parents and are attempting to drain him of all dignity as they marched him toward his inevitable death.

But amidst this hell that is his reality, Viktor has a realization so profound that it becomes a Power Belief which sustains him both during his imprisonment and for the remaining 52 years after his release. It will drive him to endure, to survive, to never give up—so that one day he might be able to teach it to the world.

Viktor Frankl described this Power Belief as thus:

Everything can be taken from a man but one thing: the last of the human freedoms—to choose one's attitude in any given set of circumstances, to choose one's own way.

His Power Belief—that man is always free to choose his attitude in any given moment, was a belief that ultimately saved Frankl's life and defined his destiny. He chose to stay empowered and optimistic. He did not let the Nazi's destroy his hope and faith in existence. Consider the magnitude of that simple belief. The Nazis can enslave me, beat me, starve me, kill my family and dehumanize me in countless ways—but I am still free to choose joy if I so desire. I can choose whatever I want. I can choose for myself regardless of external conditions. One's attitude is always an *internal*, sovereign choice. Viktor had such certainty of this truth because he was able to wield it himself, and thus his Power Belief created new beliefs such as the necessity for him to survive so he could share this insight with the rest of the world. After the war, his insight became the basis of a new branch of psychology which Viktor Frankl called Logotherapy.

In his book, *Man's Search For Meaning*, Viktor says...

When we are no longer able to change a situation, we are challenged to change ourselves.

GEORGE

In 1939, while a graduate student at UC Berkley, George Dantzig arrived late one day to his mathematics class. On the blackboard were two math problems which George assumed were homework, and so he copied them and thought nothing else about it. A few days later George returned with the homework, laid it on the teacher's desk, and apologized to his professor for taking extra time as the problems were more difficult than usual.

Six weeks later, at 8 a.m. on a Sunday, George and his wife were awakened by a ferocious banging on the front door. It was his mathematics professor. Much to Dantzig's surprise, the two problems he had turned in were not part of a homework assignment, but were in fact two famous, unsolved, statistics problems which had eluded the greatest math minds until that day. Being late, Dantzig missed the context of why they were on the board and simply assumed they were homework.

What's the power of *one* belief? Having no knowledge these were incredibly difficult, unsolved equations, Dantzig had no preconceived notion that they would be too challenging to solve. Unlike the rest of the class whose minds had been cast under a spell (belief) that these problems were impossible, Dantzig's mind simply accepted the assignment, took a couple extra days, and solved both. Let me repeat that... he solved BOTH equations!

ROGER

Roger was both a medical student and gifted runner. In 1954, Roger Bannister was enrolled at Oxford University and found himself chasing a dream that had been pursued by all world class runners for over a hundred years. His goal was to be the first man to run a mile in less than four minutes.

Twice he had attempted it and twice he had failed; his times being 4:03.6 and 4:02.0, respectively. So many men had tried the feat and failed that it became a popular notion that perhaps humans could never run a sub-four-minute mile. Rumors suggested it was due to physiological limitations; our heart, our lungs, humans just weren't biologically capable of running that fast, period. But Roger was a medical student, and with the pattern of runners shaving time off old records, getting closer and closer, he found no reason to doubt the record could be broken.

On May 6, 1954, Roger accomplished what no human had accomplished before him—he ran a mile in 3:59.4. A mere half second shy of four minutes, but it was done.

In less than a month, another human, John Landy of Australia, beat Roger's record with 3:57.9 and then, a year later, both men met on the track for a race between *giants*. When the contest was over, it was the first time in history two runners successfully ran sub-four-minute miles during the same race. Roger beat John Landy, but neither man improved on Landy's previous world record.

The significance of Roger's accomplishment was publicly likened to reaching the summit of Mt. Everest which had been accomplished for the first time in the previous year, 1953. Historical *firsts* always bring with them an infusion of legend and folklore, and such was the case with Roger's achievement. Since that May afternoon, admirers and fans have in many ways extolled his mindset as far superior than his physical ability. It was posited that Bannister did much more than simply break a speed record; he had convincingly refuted a universal limiting belief. By disproving one Power Belief, he established another. He proved that humans **are** physically able to run a sub-four-minute mile, thus freeing all future runners of any doubt in its possibility. A bevy of (then) current runners were subsequently free to accomplish what had just previously been questioned as impossible.

To counter this lore, rationalists argue that the record was bound to be broken; the pattern of steadily reduced times pointed to only one outcome—four minutes would eventually be toppled. If not Bannister, someone else. It had little to do with him having a superior mindset.

They also point to the fact that Roger knew John Landy was on his heels for the landmark feat and pressed for a May race so as not to allow Landy to set the record before him. Their position asserts that *belief* had little to do with breaking the four-minute mile.

So, what's the real story?

Did Roger Bannister free the minds of humanity by proving that man could physically run a sub-four-minute mile... or is that just *fictitious frosting* topping off an already sweet story?

Well it is true that runners had been getting progressively faster for at least a hundred years prior to Bannister's accomplishment. From 1913 until 1945 alone— the world record had dropped 13 seconds, from 4:14.4 to 4:01.4. It lingered there for nine years waiting for someone, *anyone*, to take it below the four-minute mark. For nine years runners tried in vain, Bannister included. John Landy, who broke the record less than a month after Bannister, had also been aiming at the goal and had already failed once in 1953 and three more times in early 1954. Landy's times had actually increased over his four attempts (1953 – 4:02.0 / 1954 – 4:02.2, 4:02.6, 4:02.6). On May 6, 1954, Bannister finally achieved it, and voila'— within a month, Landy did it as well. Over the next five years, 22 other runners broke the four-minute barrier. So yes, on the one hand, it seems completely reasonable to expect that someone would someday break it. On the other hand, it seems rather peculiar that so many others would achieve it, so quickly after Roger had proven it possible!

It is my opinion that what separated Roger Bannister from previous runners was not a specific Power Belief that told him it could be done, but rather the absence of a Power Belief whispering that it couldn't. And upon proving to the world it was possible, all those who may have held such a limiting belief had no reason to be imprisoned by it any longer. A mental chain had been broken. And it was Roger Bannister who broke it. Once mental chains are released, the physical world manifests all the potential that was previously blocked. It happens time and time again.

FINAL THOUGHTS: The critics who downplay the lore behind Roger Bannister's accomplishment could likewise argue that it was just a matter of time before both of George Dantzig's statistical proofs would someday be solved. This is a reasonable claim. However, in light of the fact that a single student *unwittingly* solved both math problems as a mistaken homework assignment in a span of a few days tends to prove that psychological sabotage is a real phenomenon.

The question at hand is not whether limiting beliefs exist... the productive question is how many mental roadblocks stand between us and our dreams?

What is your 4 minute mile? What is holding you back from breaking through? Is it a limiting Power Belief born from horrible circumstances, like those which plagued Viktor Frankl? Are you convinced variables you cannot control—your race, gender, religion, socioeconomic status, upbringing, geography, education, past traumas—

are insurmountable forces preventing someone in your situation from coming out the victor?

Or have you become hypnotized by the spells cast by those you conclude are *authorities* in this world? The *nay saying experts*—teachers, clergy, doctors, or family elders who have suggested your dreams are probably beyond your abilities?

Regardless of where they came from or how they got into your head, your limiting beliefs are mental chains imprisoning your potential. To break free, your task is not to find the weakest link in the chain, but rather, the strongest link. The strongest link will always be the dominating Power Belief—and once it breaks, opportunities, possibilities, and newfound abilities materialize almost instantly.

Having evidence that one single belief can either collapse or explode your destiny should now encourage each of us to investigate the unexplored world of our belief system. It is time to move forward.

The rest of this book is laid out to help you navigate the journey. Liberties were taken to help objectify something as abstract as *meaningful thought*. My goal was to establish a framework, vocabulary, and rules to demonstrate some uniform consistency across the broad expanse of human belief systems. What follows is an introduction to Belief Strategy; an effective How To resource on reprogramming your mind.

POWER BELIEFS

THE CATEGORIES, RULES, & STRATEGY OF THE GAME

If you don't change your beliefs, your life will be
like this forever. Is that good news?

~ W. Somerset Maugham

CHAPTER 3

MENTAL FENG SHUI

Before we begin, let's understand the BIG picture of what this book recommends in order for your life to open up in the direction you desire. To do that, let's discuss the concept of Feng Shui.

Feng shui is a Chinese belief system whereby the placement, arrangement, and orientation of objects within a room (let's say a living room, office, or bedroom) will then dictate the flow of energy as it travels throughout that space. Feng shui believes the arrangement of furniture can either enhance or block the flow of energy through a room. Furthermore, the flow of energy determines either favorable or unfavorable effects upon people in the room. In simplest terms: Clutter blocks energy, which in turn reduces one's positive experience.

Whether you believe in feng shui and energy flow doesn't matter. The idea that a thoughtless, haphazard arrangement of objects can clutter and reduce our positive experience is a fact we've all experienced. Disorganized toolboxes, messy closets, cluttered bookshelves, chaotic purses—these all reduce the efficiency for us to find what we seek. Clutter can cause frustration, anxiety, anger, and disappointment. In severe instances, we simply give up looking for the object.

Your mind is filled with tens of thousands, if not hundreds of thousands of beliefs. How many limiting beliefs may be cluttering up your amazing mind?—blocking the energy needed for your higher self? Convincing you to give up seeking what you truly want?

If you are like most humans, **your concept and understanding of your own belief system** is most likely in a state of disarray—if not an outright terrible (teenager bedroom) mess. For your belief system to flow and work on behalf of your dreams, you need to impose order and organization.

The first step in this process is to throw-out limiting **metabeliefs**—that is, inaccurate *beliefs about beliefs* themselves. Have you considered that you have beliefs *about* beliefs?

I have been asked if there is one pervasive, universal limiting belief shared by the majority of mankind. The question is similar to speculation on the world's most prevalent phobia. When I was younger, we were told that more people fear public speaking than do death. I'm not sure how valid that data was, and the truth is, I'm in no position to assess what single belief hampers the majority of mankind's aspirations. However, if pressed for an answer, I'd wager that an **inaccurate conceptu-alization** of our belief system is probably in the Top 10.

FIXED BELIEF SYSTEMS?

What do I mean by *inaccurate conceptualization?* It's my experience that many people conclude their belief system is like a *mental organ*—meaning it became part of them just like a liver or kidney. It's an involuntary manifestation of their being, assigned to them like a personality, or possibly a genetic result like their eye color, height, vocal tone, and base intelligence.

Sure, they feel there is a little bit of wiggle room with some of their beliefs, but ultimately, they feel it's the operating system nature programmed for them and there's very little they can do to change it.

This is a monstrous limiting Power Belief.

Rationale for such a fixed belief system goes something like this:

Beliefs emanate from my brain. My brain *thinks* similar to how my eyes *see*, my heart *beats*, and my lungs *breathe*. Yes, I can perhaps improve my vision through glasses...yes, I can increase or reduce my heart rate and breathing through exercise or relaxation—but I cannot fundamentally change what it is these organs produce. I cannot reprogram my eyes to see infrared, I cannot reprogram my lungs to breathe underwater. The same is true for beliefs that are born from my brain. My brain just thinks this way.

Others, with spiritual or religious proclivities may conclude that beliefs originate wholly outside of themselves or are an immutable part of their soul and personality.

For all those reading this who have concluded your belief systems are either genetically or spiritually fixed programs—that you had little or nothing to do with programming them—that you have little control over what you believe or why you believe it—I ask you to consider the *possibility* that this may be a flawed assessment. What would it mean for your life if you discovered this was simply a limiting metabelief, preventing you from being able to change your mindset? And if in reality I am wrong and it truly is fixed, how can you possibly harm yourself by otherwise believing it to be dynamic and fully reprogrammable? It either is, or isn't. Believing can't make it so, nor can disbelieving make it not so.

Having a dynamic belief system, which says you have absolute free will to program whatever beliefs you choose—in no way suggests such beliefs are exempt from the realities of right and wrong, true and false. Having the freedom to believe whatever you choose does not inherently validate those beliefs.

For those resistant to the idea belief systems are not fixed programs, you'll be happy to learn you do not need to accept or adopt my claim in order to gain benefit from this book. I will not be asking anyone to change any core beliefs. I will not challenge any religious convictions. In fact, everything you need to give your belief system a tune-up is already under the hood. The most effective way to modify your belief system is by using the thousands of other beliefs you already possess. That's how the advice in this book can work across such a broad swath of belief systems. There's no single "right" belief system from which we should all model our own. There are *effective* belief systems and *ineffective* belief systems.

Neither am I suggesting that external factors don't play a principle role in creating your belief system. In fact, external stimuli are what originally begins the programming process.

However, this book will continue to challenge the way you view what is happening inside your head. Our beliefs represent our view of reality and therefore we are very protective and defensive about how they are assessed, compared, or judged. But I presume the reason you are reading this book is because you're open to the idea you *can* change your beliefs. Perhaps you can readily recall dozens of times within your life you have already done so. You've most likely changed your beliefs over the course of your life on many, many topics— school, family, money, sex, politics, what's important, where mankind is heading, etc.

If you've been able to change one belief, you can change many. And as long as you believe you have the power to modify and improve your belief system, you have overcome the first hurdle.

In the feng shui spirit of better organizing our minds—
our next major cleanup is to come to an agreement of a
working definition of what a belief is in the first place. If
you think that's a simple task, Chapter 4 awaits.

CHAPTER 4

BELIEF ASSESSMENT

Having reached this point of the book, I hope we're in agreement that beliefs can either block or facilitate success in your life. However, the vital question remains: how do you eliminate Power Beliefs which block you from the life you desire? I wish there was a concise fortune cookie answer. Unfortunately, understanding HOW requires a lot more understanding of beliefs in general. It's very hard to play a game of chess (let alone win it) if you don't understand the pieces, rules, and strategies. The same is true for the components, rules, and strategies of your belief system.

Our next step is finding agreement on *what a belief actually is*, which is where things tend to get slippery, confusing, and argumentative. But if we can find agreement on what a belief is, then we are one step closer to identifying, assessing, and changing them.

So, what is a belief? Ask ten people and you're likely to get ten different answers. As our minds are filled with beliefs, as our lives are controlled by them, and as they have caused so much conflict and cruelty through-out history, one would think the average person would have a pretty concise definition of what they are. But, as you're about to find out, that is far from being the case.

- BELIEF ASSESSMENT -
CAN YOU RECOGNIZE A BELIEF?

STEP 1

Instructions: *Place a check mark beside any item that can be identified as a BELIEF. Leave non-beliefs blank.*

1. _____ Possums are reptiles

2. _____ I think I'll go workout after dinner

3. _____ It's impossible for minorities to be racist

4. _____ It's raining outside

5. _____ The sun rises in the east and sets in the west

6. _____ I assume the cop had on a bullet proof vest

7. _____ Triangles have 3 sides

8. _____ If you work hard, success is guaranteed

9. _____ I hate reading

10. _____ *"Dr. Livingston, I presume."*

11. _____ A tree has more consciousness than grass

12. _____ White owls are evil

13. _____ The sun is a nearly perfect sphere of hot plasma at the center of our solar system

14. _____ 2+2=4

15. ____ My favorite food is pizza

16. ____ I love my children

17. ____ There is either a God, or there is not. There is no other possibility.

18. ____ The speed of light is roughly 186,000 miles/second

19. ____ Area 51 is where they hide the UFO's

20. ____ Oswald killed Kennedy using karate

21. ____ Oswald didn't kill Kennedy

22. ____ For better or for worse, in sickness and in health

23. ____ Abe Lincoln was the 16th President of the U.S.

24. ____ Women are physically weaker than men

25. ____ I think, therefore I am

26. ____ That guy looks like my Uncle Tony

27. ____ My wife snores every night

28. ____ January 1st begins a new calendar year

29. ____ All Camrys are cars, but not all cars are Camrys

30. ____ Men are mortal

31. ____ Chicken soup restores health

32. ____ Columbus, Ohio is similar to Atlanta, Georgia

33. ____ We are born with ten fingers and ten toes

34. ____ I feel that nobody knows the truth

35. ____ Would you rather be rich or happy

36. ____ Becky Lustanza got nailed for copyright violation

37. ____ I have a hunch she's not coming to the wedding

38. ____ A foolish consistency is the hobgoblin of little minds

39. ____ There are only 2 cookies left in the cookie jar

40. ____ Wow, your son has really grown over the summer

How many of the 40 items did you identify
and mark as beliefs? _____

STEP 2

One of the major set-backs humans experience is
only acknowledging a belief if we, ourselves, believe
it. So, if you went through the list and only marked the
items that you felt were your own beliefs—please go
through it again and mark any you left blank that might
possibly be beliefs of others; meaning, you don't believe
the statement, but it's possible *some crazy person* might.

How many of the 40 items are now identified as beliefs? _____. Go ahead and circle that number.
This is your starting point.

STEP 3

Now go back over the items you left blank and try to
determine why you decided it was *not* a belief? This is
crucial and I caution you to not skip this step because
you need to understand **your belief about beliefs.**

STEP 4

If you are like every other person with whom I've
consulted, then you and I are about to find ourselves in
a small disagreement. I personally believe that disagree-

ments allow for the opportunity to see a different point of view if we are open-minded and inclined to do so. But perhaps we won't have a disagreement...which is likely to be the case if the total number of items you checked is 38.

Past experience would indicate your number is not 38, and most likely far fewer. It is now my job to prove that 38 of the 40 items listed can be defined as beliefs, and that is the crux of what you are about to learn in this Section. Very soon it will all make sense.

STEP 5 – BONUS POINTS

If it turns out that I can successfully explain why 38 of the 40 items can rightly be considered beliefs, which two do you think I reject as being beliefs?   #_____ and #_____.

The answers will be revealed later, because I want to give you a chance to reassess your response after you dive deeper into the core nature of beliefs.

I make this pledge: Read this entire book, give it thoughtful consideration, and by its end you will have more understanding of beliefs than every person you have met in your entire life with the slimmest chance of maybe one or two exceptions.

With your new understanding, you will be able to rid yourself of limiting Power Beliefs that are currently blocking your destiny, as well as create new Power Beliefs that propel you closer and closer toward your goals and dreams.

The only limits you have are the limits you believe.

~ Wayne Dyer

CHAPTER 5

A BELIEF =

So, what is a belief? What is the simplest definition?

be·lief —/bə'lēf/

noun   a conclusion.

That's all. Whether you conclude it's snowing outside, all pigeons can swim, 2+3=5, sudsy shampoo smells best, worms don't burp, or Earth is the 25th planet from the sun, these conclusions are beliefs. Right or wrong. Verifiable or not. All conclusions are beliefs. If something can be identified as a sincere conclusion, it's a belief.

Belief = Conclusion
Conclusion = Belief

Your beliefs—your conclusions—are simply your understandings of how reality operates and what you can therefore expect/predict from it.

Whether these conclusions about reality are true, or to what degree they are true, now becomes the most critical factor in your relationship to life, to yourself, and to others. Your conclusions can empower or limit you. They can give you peace, hatred, or madness. All that is good in the world and all that is bad—all that is possible and all that is not—is first concluded as such in our minds.

So now that we have a concise definition of what a belief is, it's time to understand why some conclusions are more powerful than others. Like pieces of a chess set, some beliefs have greater status and thus greater mental gravity within the game of life. In Chapter 6 you'll be introduced to the seven categories of beliefs which form a dominance hierarchy. Depending on which category your *dream-life* beliefs find themselves assigned, will essentially determine whether or not you'll achieve your goals.

Our ultimate strategy is to reassign the beliefs surrounding your goals and dreams to the highest-powered categories.

THE DETROIT LIONS vs. THE SUN RISE

Here's a belief: *The Detroit Lions will win next year's Super Bowl.* Here's another belief: *Tomorrow the sun will rise in the east.*

Question: Which belief gets the better odds in Las Vegas of actually happening?

You may be saying: *Wait! Hold up! The sun rising in the east is not a belief! That's a proven, scientific Fact.*

It's common for people to argue that 2+2=4 and water=H$_2$0 aren't beliefs. Individuals who make this argument have concluded (*they believe*) that "beliefs and facts" are two very different things.

However, if you examine the previous Detroit Lions and Sunrise assertions, both are undeniably conclusions.

To explore this, let's consider two more beliefs:

- *Water will freeze at 32 degrees Fahrenheit.*
- *Pandas are the cutest animals ever.*

Are they both conclusions? Yes. Then we can assert both are beliefs. But it's obvious they are very different **types** of beliefs. The first could be categorized as a Fact, while the panda conclusion is an Opinion.

For the purposes of this book, the graphic below represents the seven main **categories** of beliefs, which I will discuss in detail in Chapters 8-14. They are presented in a specific order which represents their top-down dominance hierarchy.

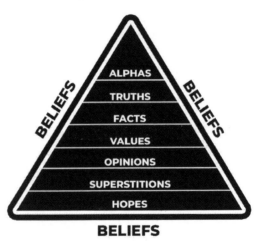

Noteworthy Digression:

Hondas and Buicks are not the same—but they are both automobiles. We might consider them *Brand Categories* of automobiles. It can be said that all Hondas are automobiles, but not all automobiles are Hondas. The same for Buicks. All Buicks are automobiles, but not all automobiles are Buicks.

I'm sure you're familiar with at least six of these category labels, and to prevent any misunderstanding as to what I'm alluding to, here are brief clarifications as to how each term relates to being a belief.

All Alphas are beliefs, but not all beliefs are Alphas

All Truths are beliefs, but not all beliefs are Truths

All Facts are beliefs, but not all beliefs are Facts

All Values are beliefs, but not all beliefs are Values

All Opinions are beliefs, but not all beliefs are Opinions

All Superstitions are beliefs, but not all beliefs are Superstitions

All Hopes are beliefs, but not all beliefs are Hopes

Expanding The Digression:

It's widely recognized that the vast majority of car accidents on an expressway are not caused by speeding, but rather by something referred to as *speed differential;* meaning the varying speeds mixing together cause accidents. When fast moving cars mix with slow moving cars, there's only a brief moment where perception and reaction times can act to prevent collisions. The greater the variance in speed, the greater chance a crash will occur.

BELIEF DIFFERENTIAL

The analogy can hold for beliefs as well. As a general rule, disagreements (social crashes) are caused by *belief differential.* Let me state that again: **Disagreements are caused by belief differential.** If disagreements are, then arguments and war as well, so belief differential is a pretty significant concept to understand. People differ on how they categorize conclusions, and when they start conversing on a common topic—crashes happen!

Most of the world's controversy comes from people arguing over category placements.

For example:

Person A believes 9/11 was an inside job; elements of the U.S. government and military helped perpetrate the attacks. For them, this conclusion is the truth. This truth springs from a cluster of other evidentiary conclusions within their belief system. Person A understands the majority of citizens do not know the "facts" needed for them to come to the same conclusion. The public is simply ignorant of the truth.

Person B believes 9/11 was orchestrated by Osama bin Laden using 19 hijackers. For them, this is the truth. Anyone who believes it was an inside job is obviously wrong because the two separate conclusions cannot both be true. They also hold additional beliefs that convince them our government doesn't do such heinous things to its own citizens. Hence, Person A's beliefs are nothing more than conspiracy theories, which Person B categorizes somewhere between Superstition and Opinion.

A & B argue this for 20 to 60 minutes, neither being able to convince the other, and typically each walking away certain the other is crazy or naive! This is category differential at play. Such scenarios are common every minute of every day on this planet. Far and away it's our belief systems that cause us the most problems; both personally and interpersonally.

Everything we hold in our mind is found somewhere on a continuum stretching across those seven categories. Those are the seven wombs of every saintly and evil act ever committed on Earth. Both philanthropy and genocide are born from beliefs. Medicine and war, competition and cooperation, religion and atheism—are all found within varying categories of a person's belief system.

Category Differential

How is knowing any of this practical? How does any of this pertain to you achieving your goals and dreams? Well here's a question: What is the likelihood you'll accomplish your dreams? Is it as certain as the sun rising in the East —or as improbable as the Detroit Lions (the only NFC team to have not yet played in the Super Bowl) winning the Super Bowl? Is your destiny a Fact, Opinion, or merely a Hope? Whatever category your destiny falls into will ultimately determine how much time, effort, and resources you'll invest in it coming true.

One of the great take-aways from reading this book will be an understanding of how belief categories differ. This insight not only allows you to identify which beliefs impact your life the most (either positively or negatively), but it will also help you change your beliefs to serve your happiness and goals. Understanding category differential will also help you understand others, why they do what they do, and which beliefs have cast a spell over their lives (for better or worse).

In the next chapters we will discuss the seven categories and how beliefs get assigned to each of them. Finally, we will learn how you can leverage these categories to your mental advantage.

CHAPTER 7

HOW YOUR MIND CATEGORIZES BELIEFS

For those unfamiliar with the "Harry Potter" series, it involves a young boy sent to a Wizard boarding school called Hogwarts. Upon arriving, new students are placed within one of the four dormitories inside the castle's campus. This is where they will live for the duration of their schooling, so placement is something akin to joining a fraternity or sorority. They are given their living arrangement during a magical ceremony wherein all new students are marched into a great hall, then called upon one-by-one to sit alone before the faculty and student body. Upon being singled out, a magic, sentient hat (called the Sorting Hat) is placed upon their head. The hat can talk and apparently reads the personality, secrets, strengths, fears, and desires of the student. By understanding and weighing these factors, the Sorting Hat wisely assigns a dormitory most fitting for the pupil.

Our minds act like the Sorting Hat when it comes to assigning beliefs to categories, and it appears to weigh three primary factors: Certainty, Consensus, and Population Affected.

To be fair and not bog you down with extraneous information, I need only cover **certainty** for you to be able to modify and improve your beliefs.

CERTAINTY

The undisputed main factor determining which category houses a belief is the level of certainty the person has regarding the conclusion. Each and every belief has a ratio of *certainty vs. doubt* in its composition. The greater the certainty, the higher it will be assigned within the belief categories. The more doubt, the lower in the categories it is placed. We call our beliefs with the highest degrees of certainty either Facts or Truths. Those with the lowest, we call Superstitions and Hopes.

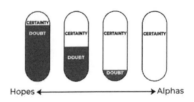

NOTE: Although certainty and doubt can be estimated by percentages (e.g. 100% certain or 63% certain, etc.) it's much easier to generalize it in the form of time/frequency. I will be using the following labels to help explain the level of certainty associated with each category:

TRUTHS - *Always True*

FACTS - *Nearly Always True*

VALUES - *Mostly True*

OPINIONS - *Sometimes True*

SUPERSTITIONS - *Seldom True*

HOPES - *Rarely, if Ever True*

This will make much more sense when we explore the individual categories and the influence each has over your belief system.

CHAPTER TAKE-AWAY

At this point it may be beneficial to realize two things about the limiting beliefs keeping your from your goals and dreams. First, whatever your limiting belief may be...

- *I'm not good enough*
- *I'll never make it*
- *It's too late for me to accomplish that*
- *I don't have the money/education/connections*

... realize you have more **certainty** in that belief than in the inverse:

- *I am good enough*
- *I will make it*
- *I have plenty of time to accomplish that*
- *I will get the money/education/connections*

See if you can identify some limiting beliefs you feel are holding you back from achieving your life goals. Write them down here:

Main Limiting Beliefs:

Upon identifying your limiting beliefs it's easy to find their inverse because it's simply the opposite. They should be stated similar to the examples on the preceding page.

Inverse Beliefs:

The second realization should be that because you have more certainty in your limiting beliefs, they would naturally be assigned to a higher category than their inverse.

With no explanation of the categories yet, do you have any sense of which categories your limiting beliefs reside? Take a guess. Remember, limiting belief must be in a higher category than their inverse, but limiting beliefs do not always find themselves in the same category.

CHAPTER 8

ALPHAS

Ultimate Cosmic Truths

A lphas are a special breed of beliefs and reign as KINGS in your belief system. They sit atop the belief hierarchy and are considered capital-T eternal Truths and can overrule any other category. Alphas are uniquely distinct from what we might refer to as scientific truths. Scientific conclusions, such as *all circles contain 360 degrees*, are divided between two other categories discussed in upcoming chapters.

Alphas are the unprovable truths involving your relationship to being alive. Beliefs in this category conclude how the universe was created, was a God or deity involved, the purpose for life, your destiny, your relationship to all other sentient life on the planet, and what happens when we die.

There is a paradoxical nature to this category. As mentioned in the previous chapter, your belief system is made up of various categories arranged in a hierarchy with the uppermost beliefs having the most **certainty** and the lower categories filled with beliefs that house more doubt. Therefore Alphas, sitting at the apex of the pyramid, should have the most certainty of any category. They should be absolutely doubt-free. But they are not.

Since Alphas are unprovable, humans are unable to possess *absolute certainty* in their truthfulness. Even the most devout go through their dark nights of questioning. Remember Jesus asking, "My God, my God, why have You forsaken me?" For those who believe in God there are many uncertainties, a simple example being—*Where did God come from?* For atheists there are also uncertainties, simple examples being—*How did life spark into being? Are we the only life forms in the universe?* For those who believe in destinies, a simple uncertainty might be—*Is this truly ordained?*

Although all of our Alphas hold doubt, we defend them as (capital T) Truths. That is the magic spell they cast upon us.

We accept they are not pure in comprehension, but we excuse that inconsistency by creating another belief which explains the doubt stems from limitations of our intelligence.

- *Our brains can't possibly fully understand God.*

- *Science hasn't discovered those answers...yet.*

I'd like to explain why I label this category ALPHAS as opposed to *worldviews* which is a much more common term. A worldview represents a person's particular philosophy of life, creation, and purpose. Alphas are the individual beliefs that help composite worldviews. Alphas are the trees, worldviews the forest. I also do not call these *religious beliefs* because that would require yet a different category for atheists. The questions answered by the Alphas (e.g. How was the universe created? Was a deity involved? What happens after death?) are the same for both theists and atheists. Same questions, different answers. I chose the term Alphas because these beliefs address the mysteries involving the origin of our existence, and they sit atop the pyramid in influence.

Here are four common Alpha Beliefs. Do you subscribe to any of these?

1. GOD created the universe and our life is a TEST which determines what happens to our soul upon death.

2. The Universe and Life are both miraculous accidents of nature – there is no purpose for being alive. There is no deity and no such thing as an after-life.

3. GOD created us, but this is not a test. There are no rights or wrongs and no rewards or punishments following the experience.

4. Life is a simulation – a complete illusionary experience. Our experience is not really life, but rather a "programmed virtual reality" that appears and feels real. It may hold meaning outside the simulation but no great profundity within.

As mentioned, clustered Alpha Beliefs create world-views. Worldviews can either include or exclude the existence of a deity. Here are nine very simplified worldviews commonly found among the population.

Which best represents your worldview?

- *Life is a sacrifice*
- *Life is a battle/struggle for survival*
- *Life is a test*
- *Life is a game*
- *Mankind is a family*
- *Life is a dream/illusion/mystery*
- *Life is a story*
- *Life is an adventure*
- *Life is a classroom*

CHAPTER TAKE-AWAY

An Alpha Belief is always considered TRUE by its adherents.

One person's Alpha may easily be categorized as a Superstition or Opinion by another.

Alpha Power Beliefs have proven to be among the mightiest forces (good and bad) on the planet. On this point, if an Alpha is opposing your dream, it will usually require finding dream-supporting Alphas to neutralize the block.

Alpha Power Beliefs are highly resistant to competing Alphas because competing Alphas are viewed as threats corrupting the Truth.

CHAPTER 9

TRUTHS

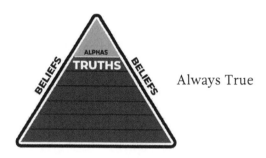

Always True

When establishing the category of Truths, it's important we introduce a distinction between the terms Truth and Fact. Our society so often conflates the two that I feel it necessary to introduce my own distinction to provide greater clarity. Please note that I am not suggesting my definitions are more correct—they simply help to understand why a belief should be assigned to one category over the other. This will help you later should you need to *play chess* with beliefs from these two categories.

Truths have zero doubt. All religions and atheists, all political parties, genders, and generations can agree that 2+2=4. And yes, 2+2=4 is a belief because it's a conclusion.

Here's a basic rule of thumb for Truths—they NEVER become untrue. They never lose their certainty. In some ways, it's impossible for them to be untrue because their defining characteristics ensure they're always true. For instance, since a triangle is literally defined as having three sides, it is impossible for it to have any other number. Should it grow another side, it is no longer a triangle by definition. A polygamist must have more than one wife or husband at the same time. Should divorce or death reduce the number of spouses to one or zero, they are simply no longer a polygamist. Like a triangle which gains an additional side, they literally become something else. Absolute certainty is built into the definitions.

Another way for a belief to be categorized as a Truth (remain permanently certain) is if the belief matter is irrevocably encapsulated by history—meaning the future universe can never undo the conclusion. For instance, as of the writing of this book, Donald Trump is the President of the United States. Is that a Fact or a Truth? Presently, one might consider it to be both, but to maximize leverage over your beliefs, to manifest your goals and dreams, it might behoove you to get into the habit of understanding this as Fact, not Truth. Truths are always certain. The word "is" in the conclusion *Donald Trump is the President of the United States* has a limited shelf-life. In 15 years, will Donald Trump still be the President of the United States? No. Even if Donald Trump somehow seized dictatorial powers to remain in office after any duly elected term, he will eventually die and not be President. The certainty that Donald

Trump *IS* the President is guaranteed to change with the passage of time. In 15 years will 2+2=4? In 1,000 years will triangles still have three sides? What will remain true is that Donald Trump *was* the 45th President of the United States. That is sealed in history and cannot be changed. That will always be a Truth. *Change* is the primary difference between a Truth and a Fact. Facts can change.

CHAPTER TAKE-AWAY

A truthful conclusion (belief) will <u>never</u> change.

None of our beliefs in the remaining five categories will possess the quality of *always* being true. They are assigned to categories based on how frequently we can be certain of their truthfulness. The more certain a person is in the conclusion not changing, the higher up in the categories it is placed. The less certain they are, the lower its overall value.

This is how humans are: we question all our beliefs, except for the ones we really believe, and those we never think to question.

~ Orson Scott Card

CHAPTER 10

FACTS

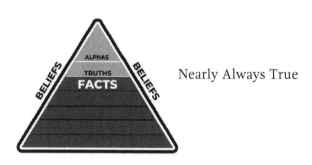

Nearly Always True

Facts possess the second-highest level of certainty. However, Facts are a category that allows for deviation and change. Examples? It was once considered a Fact that *Pluto is our 9th planet*. Not now. It has been downgraded to being a dwarf planet and was subsequently kicked out of the starting line-up. Is the belief that the United States is comprised of 50 states a Truth or a Fact? Might that number change—either up or down? If so, it's a Fact. Unlike a Truth whose certainty is permanent, the certainty of a Fact is not permanent over time or context.

Consider this Fact: As of the writing of this sentence, the fastest time ever recorded for running a full marathon is 1:59:40. Currently, that is a Fact. But will that stay a Fact for all of eternity? Might someone else set the fastest record someday, and then that new record becomes a Fact? Facts allow for change.

Even science allows for exceptions to certainty via the p-value within the statistical measuring of a hypothesis. When testing a hypothesis, scientists are not expected to reap 100% certainty in the results. Previously I introduced the universal conclusion that water will freeze at 32 degrees Fahrenheit. Is this a Truth or is this a Fact? Does water *always* freeze at 32 degrees Fahrenheit? No. The freezing point of water decreases in temperature as pressure increases. The more pressure exerted on water, the colder it needs to be for water to freeze. Facts allow for exceptions.

FLEX-FACTS

To again demonstrate how we allow Facts to be both certain and fleeting, let's imagine we meet on a street corner and you ask me for the time. I look at my watch and proclaim it's 2:11 p.m. Although it may factually be 2:11 p.m. where we both stand, both of us accept it is not 2:11 p.m. in other time zones, nor will it stay 2:11 for much longer. We allow Facts to be contextual and extremely temporal.

All this may sound like technical semantics and intellectual hair-splitting. But when it comes to realizing your dreams, there is a huge difference in whether something blocking your dreams is a Truth (which will never change), or a Fact, which could change simply depending on where you stand on the planet.

Most people wrongfully assume Facts are Truths, and then cast the poisonous spell that their life can never change.

I have no business experience, I don't have the right connections, I have no money... yes, all those are Facts. The great news is, Facts can change. Pluto is no longer a planet—and you no longer must remain a victim of mis-categorized beliefs!

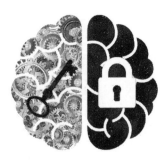

The world we see that seems so insane is the result of a belief system that is not working. To perceive the world differently, we must be willing to change our belief system.

~ William James

CHAPTER 11

VALUES

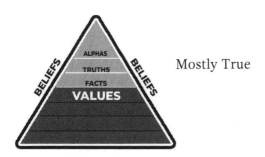

Mostly True

Values have a very strong, downstream relationship to one's Alpha beliefs. They are usually defined in terms of the attitudes and behaviors needed to insure one's worldly happiness and success. They often conclude how we should treat other people and the world at large.

Value conclusions tend to have causality built into them. Values are like unspoken if-then statements. They are not always expressed as such, but upon analyzing them, causality is clearly understood.

Examples of Values include:

Honesty is the best policy

A stitch in time saves nine

Hard work pays off

Spare the rod and spoil the child

Values serve as our unpublished rule book, guiding us away from ruin toward a happier life.

But, we also understand and accept that Values aren't always true. We occasionally doubt them delivering on their promises. For example, take the Value **Honesty is the Best Policy**—the subtext being, things always turn out better if you're honest. So, the question now is, does the holder of this conclusion have certainty this is always the case? Are there ever instances where telling the truth can cause things to turn out worse than if one just lies?

If you were hiding Jews from the Nazis in the 1930s and the Gestapo came knocking asking if you knew of anyone hiding Jews—honesty is a really bad choice at this moment. Also, I wouldn't advise being honest with an anonymous Nigerian emailer who is asking for your bank account number. I'm sure there are many more examples to show that honesty is not always the best policy, but if we accept it as being true *most of the time*, it's categorized as a Value.

Let's explore the Value **Hard Work Pays Off**. Expressed in its if-then form, it becomes, *If you work hard, you will then succeed.* Is there absolute certainty of this claim? Absolutely not. Billions of people around the world work very hard only to find themselves languishing in poverty. Slaves work very hard. Does the conclusion rise to the level of Fact, which is *nearly always true*? That would depend upon one's definition of the term success, but I believe confidence wanes below the level of nearly always true. There are so many other variables to contend with besides one's work ethic...how many businesses failed due to the 2020 Covid-19 pandemic? Was that due to lack of hard work?

Is it true *most of the time,* that if you work hard, you'll succeed? If you agree with that conclusion, then it's likely this is one of your Values. If you do not agree with that conclusion, this most likely becomes an **Opinion.** For instance, a person who identifies as an oppressed minority may agree that hard work *should* pay off most of the time—but when coupled with other conclusions in their belief system (i.e. systemic racism thwarts minorities from achieving success regardless of how hard they work), this is no longer a Value for them. Their belief may default to *Sometimes Hard Work Pays Off.* In such a case, the belief **Hard Work Pays Off** gets downgraded to another category whose beliefs are merely *sometimes* true. We call those Opinions.

CHAPTER TAKE-AWAY

As Values conclude how we should think and behave in order to live a successful life, it's an almost given that your ultimate goals and dreams are connected to your Values— either in a positive or negative relationship.

Values are where a lot of dreams are sacrificed. They are sacrificed for the preservation of other competing Values. It's a trade-off which seems to make sense, but can actually derail you from living your happiest, most successful life.

For example, let's assume fictitious Kelly, once dreamed of being a college professor. In high school she unexpectedly lost a parent, and like many children in this predicament, she developed a limiting belief that her own life may get cut short. One of Kelly's Alpha beliefs concludes *old age is promised to no one* and so her downstream Values promoted and elevated a conclusion that *life should be not be wasted or taken for granted.* For her, because she may die young, living a successful life requires her to experience as much joy and happiness as possible. Adopting this as a top Value directly downgrades other values such as hard work and sacrifice. Joy and happiness are more important than "accomplishment" because she may not live long enough to experience career success or realize complex, time-driven goals.

Clustered alongside her *live for the moment* Values are related beliefs such as: *relationships are more important than dreams, life experience and travel provide a more meaningful education than college,* as well as *immediate gratification is better than delayed gratification.*

Now in her mid-thirties, Kelly is underemployed, out of shape, and becoming more estranged from her group of friends who are preoccupied with their own careers and families. She feels alone, unsuccessful, and too old to start over.

Given her subconscious programming, Kelly did everything right. She leveraged an Alpha Power Belief (*no one is guaranteed old age*) to establish Values (*one should live for now*) that prioritized her behaviors to ensure she would lead a successful life. But the programming was specific for a life ending prematurely.

Unfortunately, Kelly's is a sad example proving Values are only *Mostly True*.

The real culprit however was the limiting Power Belief *(I may die young)* that held reign over her Values and continued her down a narrowing path. Kelly wrongly categorized this as an Alpha Belief. Remember, Alpha Beliefs (1) deal with issues such as our fate and purpose in life—(2) they are, for the most part, unprovable, and (3) deemed Ultimate Cosmic Truths. So, believing she would die young (fate) without being able to prove she would live to an old age, birthed a limiting Power Belief which she subconsciously categorized as an Alpha, and thus a Cosmic Truth. It doesn't go higher than that.

Unless Kelly's parent died of an untreatable, hereditary disease of which she was also diagnosed, the certainty of her or any human dying young (in modern civilization) is nowhere near *Always True*, *Nearly Always True*, or even *Mostly True*. Her belief should have been categorized as *Sometimes True* (Opinion) or *Seldom True* (Superstition). Such awareness would have offered broader options for her path forward. Now in her mid-thirties, Kelly is finally doubting the belief that she will die young, but, unfortunately, seems to be replacing that with another limiting Opinion—namely, that *she is too old to start over.*

CHAPTER EXERCISE

If you truly want to improve your life and better the odds of realizing your dreams, do not simply accept these chapters as perfunctory information.

You have Alphas and Values tied directly to your goals and dreams. Does your mind accept these goals as being aligned with your highest purpose? Or are these dreams at odds with your Values? Will accomplishing your goals require *long hours* or *overthrowing the competition* when you have more dominant Values that tell you *time with your family* or *kindness* are more important?

Consider your top Values. These would be the RULES you've adopted as necessary to have a good and successful life. List your Top Five. And then circle any you feel are interfering with, or at least causing friction with attitudes and behaviors necessary to accomplish your goals.

1.

2.

3.

4.

5.

CHAPTER 12

OPINIONS

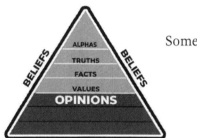

Sometimes True

This is the tipping point category. This is where beliefs start to get cloudy and really confuse people. When you get to Opinions, the lines between categories start to blur and category differential becomes more of an issue.

In some ways, Opinions aren't even considered beliefs, they're generally thought of as preferences, such as *my favorite food is pizza,* or *I prefer cream in my coffee,* or *I'd rather sit on the aisle than beside the window.* However, each of the aforementioned preferences is a conclusion.

Whereas Alphas, Truths, and Facts seem deprecated when someone casually refers to them as a belief, Opinions are typically valued as something even *less than a belief...* something akin to a transient whimsy.

One clue to identifying Opinions is the personalization ascribed to each conclusion—*my favorite is, I prefer, I think, I would rather,* etc. It's generally recognized that Opinions are personal conclusions. That's one of the benchmark indicators establishing the *Sometimes True* designation. Because no matter the conclusion, for certain people on the planet, it's sometimes true. A conclusion may only pertain to one single person and only for a limited amount of time, e.g. *that's my favorite song!* The belief-holder doesn't expect others should believe the same thing. This is another clue that a belief is an Opinion. If people argue over Opinions—most likely those are miscategorized beliefs.

There seems to be three scenarios befalling an encounter with someone else's Opinion.

Opinion Agreement – you agree with the other person's conclusion. *Wow! I also like Piña Coladas and getting caught in the rain!*

Soft Disagreement – you disagree with the person but find nothing objectionable about their conclusion. *Cats are okay, but I'm more of a dog person.*

Contentious Disagreement – the other person's Opinion is found to be insulting and/or objectionable, usually to the point where you feel the need to counter and argue it, such as—*I couldn't disagree more! Violent felons should never be able to own firearms!* Such disagreements are a clue the "Opinion" has been miscategorized.

WHEN OPINIONS CAUSE CONFLICTS

Rarely do people feel the need to argue with or edify someone who proclaims, "*I hate lemon yogurt,*" or "*I prefer to eat scrambled eggs with ketchup.*" Others don't usually process these conclusions as threatening to their assessment of reality. They are correctly interpreted as Opinions—as personal preferences, as conclusions that are *Sometimes True.*

Even when another's personal preference contradicts our own, we seldom feel our reality is threatened. "*You couldn't give me an Iphone—I'm a loyal Android user*" or "*There's nothing sexier than a Redhead!*"

Opinions become contentious when they trespass into the higher categories—Values, Facts, Truths, and Alphas. Once you cross the personal preference corridor, you've entered territory that affects many others, possibly everyone. In that regard, it's difficult to hear contrary conclusions and not feel our reality is threatened. Here are a few examples of when conclusions trespass into other belief categories while still masquerading as personal Opinions:

> *It's my Opinion that women should stay home and take care of the children.* [Actually deals with *Mostly True* **Values**]

> *It's my Opinion that XY chromosomes and a penis have nothing to do with making you a male.* [Actually deals with *Nearly Always True* **Facts**]

> *It's my Opinion that a student's math creativity is more important than getting the correct answers.* [Actually deals with *Always True* **Truths**]

It's my Opinion that everyone who's not a (fill in religious affiliation) will burn in a fiery hell. [Actually deals with *Eternal Cosmic Truths* **Alphas**]

As you can tell, these beliefs are not really Opinions but conclusions of higher categories. As such, they open the door for conflict. A current malaise in the United States involves political discord. Political "Opinions" get a great deal more argument because they directly deal with how we should treat other people and manage the world at large. In other words, Values, Facts, and Alphas. As mentioned in the previous chapter, Values relate to Alphas, so whenever you insult a downstream Value, it's likely that you're also insulting an upstream Alpha. As an example, think of the political divide regarding Climate Change. Each side quarrels over the priority of the Values involved (environment vs. economy), the legitimacy of Facts involved (man-made vs. natural), and even Alphas (we'll survive vs. extinction crisis.) *Ketchup on your eggs* doesn't affect me. Laws that dictate my freedoms and survival do! The claws come out because both sides feel threatened.

Consider the issue of abortion. Is one's stance merely a *Sometimes True* Opinion? Let's analyze two general statements aligned with views from each camp.

Pro-Life: *It's my Opinion, abortion is murdering a baby.*

Pro-Choice: *It's my Opinion, abortion is not murdering a baby; it's simply preventing a clump of cells from becoming a baby.*

Each statement is voiced as an Opinion, but think of all the implicit, underlying categories involved.

Values – How should one handle unwanted pregnancy, and who gets to choose?

Facts – How does one define murder?

Truth – When does life actually start?

Alpha – How does murder vs. forced term delivery align or conflict with one's Worldview?

CHAPTER TAKE-AWAY

How does understanding Opinions affect your personal success and destiny? As mentioned in the opening of this chapter, Opinions are where lines of categories start to blur. It's this blurring phenomena that can get you in trouble. We've seen how conflict arises when someone tries to trespass into our higher categories with a conflicting personal Opinion. But the reverse often occurs and can be quite devastating. Oftentimes, we categorize something as a Fact when it's merely another's personal Opinion.

Our belief system is littered with Opinions masquerading as Facts and Truths and Alphas. Early childhood through our teen years are stained with miscategorized Opinions from our parents, teachers, and peers. The majority of criticisms we've faced in our life have been Opinions posing as something more. We internalized these and grounded them in levels of certainty way beyond *Sometimes True*.

We are also deceived by our own Opinions, believing certain skills and achievements are beyond our abilities, certain people won't find value in us, people our age or from our socio-economic level can't make it. All Opinions...and only *sometimes true*.

It's very likely the majority of your disappointments and failures are rooted in wrongly categorized Opinions. In Chapter 21, "The Force Field," I'll explain why our minds are so resistant to simply downgrade or eliminate these beliefs, but it's my experience that in the feng shui clutter of your mind, Opinions (your own and others') are a hoarding disorder blocking your goals and dreams.

CHAPTER 13

SUPERSTITIONS

Seldom True

The term Superstition is absolutely loaded with negative connotations and is bound to get a lot of push back as being the label for this category. I'm hopeful you'll bear with me a couple pages and allow me to explain why I believe the category deserves this label more so than any other. This category is filled with beliefs that are seldom true; so seldom, in fact, some may never be true.

Superstitions are often associated with beliefs like the following:

A black cat crossing your path brings bad luck

If you find a four leaf clover, it will bring you good luck

Breaking a mirror delivers seven years back luck

A rabbit's foot brings you good luck

Walking under a ladder brings bad luck

Crossing your fingers brings you good luck

If you spill the salt you need to take a pinch and throw it over your right shoulder to prevent bad luck

Knocking on wood prevents jinxing your good luck

Full moons and Friday the 13th are bad luck

Hanging a horseshoe over the door brings good luck

A groom seeing the bride before the ceremony brings bad luck

Find a penny pick it up – all day long you'll have good luck

Opening an umbrella indoors brings bad luck

Wishing upon a star brings about the wish

Blowing out candles on the birthday cake brings about the wish

Breaking a wishbone brings good luck to the one who gets the larger portion

Central to all these beliefs is the intervention of "luck" —a mysterious, supernatural force that delivers fortune or misery not because of your actions, but because some paranormal sequence has been activated.

More common examples are found in the arenas of sports and gambling.

Example:

Gary is a 32-year-old white collar professional who believes he recently discovered a way to hack cosmic causality. It seems that every time he wears his cheese-stained lucky jersey, coupled with his team being an underdog, coupled with watching the game at Trevor's house...his team wins!

Seriously! It has happened twice so far!! Gary has connected these seemingly random conditions and notices this coupling magically *produces* a win for his team. There is no reasonable cause-and-effect for Gary to explain the phenomena, but nonetheless he has a superstitious conclusion that these conditions help his team win. Therefore, the jersey will remain unwashed until the universe figures out he's discovered the hack and patches it.

Gambling is a Mecca of Superstitions. Why? Because the conclusions we wish to happen (us winning!) are *seldom true*. The odds of three cherries showing up on the slot machine, the dice combo landing a seven, or our team covering the spread were designed to be *seldom true*. But the bookies are smart—as certainty decreases, payouts increase. This entices humans to invent strange beliefs that somehow flip certainty back to our favor.

Luck is the mysterious, invisible force that swoops in to deliver that certainty. Lucky coins, lucky shirts, a beautiful woman blowing on the dice, specific mantras—these are the magic elements that bend reality to our favor. But you know what?—people definitely win against the odds, and that's why this category is defined as being *seldom true*. Seldom doesn't mean never.

Luck, however, isn't reserved for monetary outcomes alone.

Something old, something new, something borrowed, something blue.

That is a Superstition which concludes four items incorporated into a bride's wedding outfit will deliver her a good marriage. Again, some outside mysterious force uses those objects to ensure health, wealth, and happiness for the newlyweds going forward. However, it's unclear if that good fortune is then cancelled by bad mojo should the groom glimpse his bride on their wedding day before she walks down the aisle. (Yet to be determined!)

CHAPTER TAKE-AWAY

Do you believe that in order for your goals and dreams to come true, you need an unbelievable amount of good luck?

Do you believe the reason you haven't succeeded with your dreams is because of bad luck?

If you're relying solely on luck to succeed it's likely due to a limiting beliefs (probably fears) surrounding the actions necessary for you to plow ahead and capture your destiny. Because you may not want to do what is needed—like taking big risks or stepping outside your comfort zone—you replace responsibility and necessity of action with luck swooping in and handing you your destiny. This is a terrible strategy. Dreams based on luck are *seldom true*. You need to replace limiting beliefs that are imprisoning you inside your comfort zone with empowering beliefs that motivate you forward.

Although all Superstitions are *seldom true*, there is one more category that has even less frequency of being true... it's called HOPE.

CHAPTER 14

HOPES

Lloyd: Just give it to me straight. The least you can do is
level with me. What are my chances?
Mary: Not good.
Lloyd: You mean...not good, like one out of a hundred?
Mary: I'd say more like... one out of a million.
Lloyd: So you're telling me there's a chance!!

~ Scene from the 1994 movie "Dumb & Dumber"

Rarely, if Ever True.

Hopes have the lowest certainty of any category. They
are almost the inverse of Facts. Whereas Facts are
loaded with certainty but allow for minor exceptions to the
rule, Hopes are loaded with doubt, always praying for a minor exception to the rule.

The certainty of not winning the lottery, of not recover-
ing from stage four cancer, of not being rescued when my
boat capsizes at sea—such overwhelming and discomfort-
ing odds is the fountainhead of Hope beliefs. When the
odds are against us and we can't find a reasonable solution,

instead of surrender, we holdout and allow for the possibility of supernatural forces or statistical anomalies coming to our rescue. Depending on our Alpha beliefs, these supernatural forces either come in the form of luck, God's intervention, or both. Luck and God are both capable of pulling off longshots. If they happen, we call them miracles!

It's a miracle we won!

It's a miracle I'm still alive!

It's a miracle we were found!

Perhaps you believe that Hope is not a belief, but rather a wish and thus should not be included in this book as a category. But underlying every wish is at least one conclusion which makes it a belief.

Examples of common conclusions underlying our Hopes:

I hope to win the lottery!
Playing my kids' birthdates will allow me to win the Powerball.

I hope I survive cancer!
Praying to God will cure my cancer.

I hope we're rescued at sea!
God will save us... He won't let our family drown.

Note: You may be asking, what's the difference between Hope and Superstition when it comes to the lottery and luck? They are both gambling. Shouldn't they be the same category? The short answer is—it all depends on the odds. I have placed them in different categories based on the odds of them being true. You will win more frequently in Vegas (seldom) playing whatever your game-of-chance turns out to be, than you will with the Powerball Lottery (rarely, if ever).

Final thoughts: If your life's dreams find themselves currently rooted in the category of Hope, do not despair. As mentioned, Hopes are like Facts; neither has absolute certainty, so both can change. And I have not yet begun explaining how to reprogram your beliefs to increase their certainty.

- SECTION SYNOPSIS -

The power of any belief is directly related to whichever category it finds itself assigned. As explained in this section, we categorize beliefs by the relative frequency of their conclusions being true. The **certainty** we have in them being *true*.

A belief the sun will rise again tomorrow? Thus far, always true; I'll bet everything I have on it.

A belief the Detroit Lions will win next year's Super Bowl? Thus far, never true, which gives me certainty they won't win.

Certainty is also directly related to your emotional motivation. High certainty inspires proactive, emotional motivation. Low certainty suppresses motivation. For example: the conclusion that my house IS on fire right this minute—that level of certainty inspires an incredible amount of motivation to flee the house and save my life. The conclusion that a terrorist attack WILL destroy my city (which I currently weigh as possible, but rarely, if ever true) doesn't inspire me to pack up and move elsewhere. This analogy holds regarding your goals and dreams, as well. If you believe your dreams are merely Hopes, long shots, *sometimes true, seldom true, rarely if ever true*—you will not conjure the emotional motivation necessary to do what needs to be done to succeed. All achievement and success require some form of activity. From losing weight, to starting a business, to finding your soulmate, to curing cancer—before any of those can be accomplished you must first invest time and activity. However, as biological creatures, we are instinctively programmed to conserve energy. Humans refrain from burning calories on activities with iffy conclusions.

Question: As of this moment, which category best describes the confidence you have in your dreams coming true?

TRUTHS - *Always True*
FACTS - *Nearly Always True*
VALUES - *Mostly True*
OPINIONS - *Sometimes True*
SUPERSTITIONS - *Seldom True*
HOPES - *Rarely, if Ever True*

If you answer anything less than *Mostly True* (Values), you'll need to increase your certainty to unleash proactive emotional motivation. You need to hitch your dream to the highest categories. I'll show you how.

POWER BELIEFS

WHERE DO BELIEFS
COME FROM AND WHY?

We are born believing.
A man bears beliefs as a tree bears apples.

~ Ralpha Waldo Emerson

CHAPTER 15

ORIGINS OF YOUR BELIEFS

So where did these thousands upon thousands of con-clusions come from? How do legitimate conclusions with high certainty find themselves mixed with illegiti-mate, limiting beliefs? Does a belief's *origin* offer any clues as to how it attained certainty and placement within a cat-egory? Can its origin help us either strengthen or weaken the conclusion?

It would be impossible to understand the origin of all our beliefs, (as we have so many and they were formed so long ago) but for those beliefs which limit us in the most significant ways, it's probable that we can at least narrow-in on how they were imparted to our mind. All our limiting beliefs were at some point planted, through some means. Determining their birth mothers can provide great insight as to their objective certainty. Therefore, having a general understanding of how beliefs manifest, can help us both weaken limiting beliefs and strengthen empowering be-liefs.

There are six prominent root causes that feed the creation of your belief system. We'll explore three of them in this chapter and the remaining three in chapters 16-18.

DIRECT EXPERIENCE

"No teacher is greater than one's own experience."
~ W. Timothy Gallwey

The first and absolutely most powerful root cause is Direct Experience, wherein you have formulated the conclusion through your own sensory experience of the world. Simple examples of beliefs created by Direct Experience are: ice cream tastes good, rocks are hard, night follows day, Grandma's kitchen smells like soup.

The problem with direct experience is that our senses are often faulty and misleading. We are fooled all the time by optical illusions, fragments of conversations and memories, distance, and perspective. One only needs to spend a few minutes with a deft magician to realize our subjective experience isn't the whole story.

However, direct personal experience is the baseline we each trust when confronted with opposing beliefs. When conclusions clash, we are much more prone to believe our own experience than something that contradicts our experience. To highlight the conviction of direct experience, here is a resounding example.

If every person in the entire world—scientists, artists, friends and family alike, told you that neither color nor sound exists, would it be possible for you to accept this conclusion?

AUTHORITY DOWNLOAD

A second means of belief creation is through Authority Download whereby conclusions are inherited by sources you deem credible; parents, siblings, teachers, Big Bird on Sesame Street, etc. At the time you adopted these beliefs, you either had no first-hand experience about such conclusions, or the authority's conclusions simply provided you with more certainty. Examples are: *Abe Lincoln was our 16th President, Earth is the 3rd planet from the sun, eight comes after seven,* and *all reptiles are cold blooded.*

Most people adopt their religious, political, and Value beliefs from their parents, who in turn adopted them from their own. Like Direct Experience, there are also many problems with Authority Downloads. Spoiler alert: humans are frequently wrong. Super frequently, and super wrong! How many millions upon millions of thwarted dreams have there been throughout history, foiled perhaps by a single comment from a parent, spouse, or friend in which the person was told—*that'll never happen, you're not smart enough, not talented enough, not experienced enough*? How many countless might-have-been artists, inventors, teachers, doctors, leaders, humanitarians, etc. has the world missed out on by faulty, limiting beliefs downloaded from an authority source?

EXTRAPOLATION

A third means of developing beliefs is through Extrapolation, wherein you derive new conclusions based on other beliefs you have already accepted. The following are two examples presented in very different manners to help you understand extrapolated beliefs.

Example 1:

Belief: *I don't like cold weather* (Direct Experience)

Belief: *The continent of Antarctica is cold* (Authority Download)

Belief: *I'd hate visiting Antarctica* (Extrapolation)

Example 2:

It was difficult watching Mary burn at the stake, but Reverend Goodheart said she was a witch, so a witch she must be (Authority Download). Who are we to question the validity of his education and wisdom in such matters? As the Reverend testified at her trial, he's twice witnessed her conversing aloud as she walked alone through the forest (Direct Experience). And people converse with other entities, not themselves (Direct Experience). Evil spirits are invisible (Authority Download/Extrapolation)—so Mary must've been carrying on with evil spirits because there was no one else around (Extrapolation). Therefore, Mary is undoubtedly a witch (Extrapolation).

Unfortunately, our minds weave such faulty and pernicious extrapolations all the time. We believe, not that we
are witches, but rather incapable, undeserving, uneducat-
ed, unattractive, unlovable.
These inner extrapolations
are Power Beliefs that hold
back most humans. They are
the knots in our belief system that choke our potential
success and fulfillment. It is
therefore the job of every understanding person to untan-

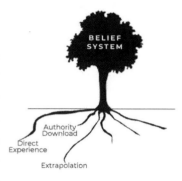

gle the harmful knots they have woven into their beliefs.
Understanding how your belief system was programmed
is an extremely important step in untangling these knots.

CHAPTER EXERCISE

To better help you understand your limiting beliefs and
how you may have come about investing certainty in their
conclusions, let's do a little thought experiment.

Let's imagine there actually exists a magic belief wand—
which **can only take away limiting beliefs.** So you wave
this magic wand and you're able to clear 5 Limiting Beliefs.
*Which 5 beliefs, if they were no longer in your head, would
help you the most toward pursuing and actually realizing your
goals?*

If you're having difficulty coming up with limiting beliefs, determine if you have beliefs pertaining to your goals
and dreams that fit any of the following formulas:

- I can't _____.

- I don't have _____.

- If I didn't have to do _____.

See if any limiting beliefs come to your mind. When you feel you've found 5 very strong limiting beliefs, list them below.

1.

2.

3.

4.

5.

- DIRECT EXPERIENCES -

List any direct experience you have that may have helped create those limiting beliefs.

- AUTHORITY DOWNLOADS -

Quickly run through your memory and see if any authority figures —adults, teachers, coaches, doctors, bosses, pop to the forefront of your memory for being negative influencers on your abilities and/or dreams. Can you recall any insults, *reality-check* pep talks, or even subtle non-verbals that let you know they thought you couldn't accomplish your goals and dreams?

Make notes of limiting Authority Downloads you may have adopted from these influencers.

- EXTRAPOLATIONS -

Do any of the Top 5 limiting beliefs you listed on page 86 seem to be Extrapolations? Meaning, you have probably created this belief by combining 2 or more other beliefs? Can you defend why you have certainty toward these beliefs?

If you have a limiting belief that concludes—*It's too late for me to (fill in the blank)*—determine what other beliefs are combining to form such a conclusion. What makes it too late? How do you know this? Is this a *sometimes true* belief that you've mistaken as a *nearly always true* belief?

If you have a limiting belief that concludes—**I** *don't have the money needed to (fill in the blank)*—is the real underlying conclusion simply (a) *you can't think of how to earn more money,* or that (b) *you don't want to give up your evenings, and weekends to get a second job?* Maybe you're a single parent and can't work a second job, which would cause us to rephrase your limiting belief as (c) *I'm unable to get a higher paying job,* or (d) *I don't know how to get a higher paying job.* Get very clear WHERE the limitation actually is.

Tear apart your limiting beliefs and find out what other beliefs give each one power? What other beliefs would cause someone to believe they can't get a higher paying job?

Ask of each limiting belief, "HOW might somebody else in your situation overcome this?" Then ask why you can't do the same? This answer will most likely point to a limiting Power Belief. Bingo!

The next time your core beliefs are challenged -
try being curious instead of furious.

~ Randy Gage

CHAPTER 16

REPETITION

Imagine yourself on a tropical beach swaying in a hammock strung between two palm trees. Your best friend is there swinging beside you, both of you watching the clouds. What eventually happens is you notice a shape and most likely some shading contours, and—PRESTO—you see it! You point and ask your friend, *"Hey, doesn't that cloud look like (fill in the blank)?"*

If they see it too, it somehow feels like a victory for both of you. If they don't, you spend a good amount of time explaining it to them. *"See the tail over there? And that thing is the eye..."* Perhaps now they say, *"Yeah—okay, now I see it!"*, and again, it's a win. If they're still squinting a minute later, they don't see it, and it's now probable that they can no longer see it because the winds have changed the formation. And for some reason you feel disappointed. For some reason it feels like a failed opportunity to agree upon some aspect of external reality.

91

We do this quite often with our beliefs as well. We tend to associate, befriend, marry, and enjoy people who share our same beliefs. We say something, they agree, and congratulations! Our assessment of reality seems to be validated. We'll discuss this later when we explore confirmation bias, but for now let's return to what's happening on the beach.

Cloud watching exemplifies perhaps the most fantastic ability we have as conscious, intelligent beings. Nearly everything you know is built on a remarkable ability to recognize patterns; and the essential ingredient of every pattern is repetition. Repetition is (for lack of a better way to emphasize its significance) the **central cog** in your belief factory. Repetition creates certainty. Certainty creates conviction.

When you were one to three years old, your toddler brain began recognizing patterns of sounds at astonishing rates. *Doggie* and *Daddy* at first sounded the same—but over time, through repetition, you were able to differentiate those sound vibrations into two very different words with two very different meanings. Through repetition, sounds became more and more recognizable. Not just the literal words, but the nonverbal nuances that offered conclusions as well. Your name spoken loud and angrily was a pattern that concluded one thing... your name spoken in a high pitched, almost lilting rhythm concluded something else. You were able to determine through sound alone whether it was your father, mother, or sibling calling you from the other room—as well as whether they were happy, frightened, or angry.

Eventually with enough exposure to repeating patterns, you were also able to decode meaningful patterns like accents and dialects, or even complex concepts like sarcasm and sincerity. So many conclusions from the nuances of sound waves; fluctuations in pitch, volume, rapidity, tonality, and duration. It was all put together through pattern recognition. What an amazing ability!

Let's not forget Touch. There is a forgotten moment in your childhood when the meaning of *smooth* totally sank into your comprehension. You had felt it enough times and were told at those moments that such a perception was known as smooth and.... *Ahh, I get it! That means SMOOTH.* And since then, every time your fingers or skin experienced that same tactile pattern, you understand its conclusion as smoothness. Alongside smoothness, you also came to understand the patterns of roughness, sliminess, dryness, prickliness, softness, hardness, wetness, hotness, and coldness. These are not only sensations, these are conclusions!

Repetition of smells allowed you to confidently differentiate between bacon and gasoline. Smoke was an olfactory pattern that signaled potential danger. How about salty, sweet, and spicy? They are all taste patterns. At what age would you have successfully been able to identify apples versus pears by taste alone?

Conclusions, conclusions, conclusions.

And so, we continued to devour and process stimuli, searching for patterns, refining patterns, cross-testing patterns. All the patterns that were identified, along with the conclusions we associated with them, took their meaningful place within one of the categories of our belief system.

Spring turns to Summer then to Fall and then Winter.

Shaking a soda can then opening it makes a mess.

Whenever I hold a door open for someone, they smile or thank me.

That song always makes my mother cry.

Roasted marshmallows are sticky.

You would not be able to understand what I am writing were it not for your amazing ability to recognize symbolic patterns. The Alphabet is comprised of 26 different shapes we call letters. Using only curves and straight lines to fashion these symbols, it eventually sank in that this was a *C* and this was a *G*. The patterns could vary slightly, and you'd still recognize them. This was an *O* and this was a *Q*. Eventually, the following patterns all became known as variations of the same thing - A a *A* **A** **A** *A* *A* **A** *A* **A** **A** *A* @

On and on, belief after belief, conclusion after conclusion, until your mind turned into a never-ending belief factory. Pattern recognition is mankind's superpower, built from one single phenomenon: Repetition. Repetition is the foundation on which our understanding of reality is built.

CHAPTER 17

COMPARE AND CONTRAST

Many of our beliefs, especially those rooted in our identity, worth, and self-respect, were created through the process of comparison. Growing up, we eventually realize we are judged by our appearance, our humor, our intelligence, our clothing, our family's social status, our religion, our talents and personality—all in comparison with others in our community, and we form Power Beliefs based solely on these comparisons. These beliefs can be either positive or negative depending on the outcome of the comparison, but oftentimes they simply limit us.

Lest we think the construction of self-identity is a once-and-done phenomenon, a process limited to one's childhood, it's important to realize comparisons continue and beliefs change throughout life. A single-digit millionaire no longer feels wealthy when

he attends a conference with decamillionaires who own G5 private jets. A woman watches as a younger couple at a restaurant paw and swoon over each other and concludes her 20-year marriage is perfunctory and loveless. A famous actor wonders why, although nominated several times, he never wins the Oscar. Comparisons are constantly shaping our conclusions about ourselves and the world.

In his book "David vs. Goliath," Malcolm Gladwell explores the fluidity of self-esteem and confidence when top students from various high schools later find themselves competing with thousands of brilliant peers at Harvard. Countless students who desired a math or science degree no longer find themselves in the top percentiles of candidates and must change majors—literally changing the course/destiny of their lives. Because they can't compete at Harvard, they simply drop the career goals they once desired. You may assume this simply illustrates the very-smart comparing themselves with the uber-smart and giving up. However, that is not the significant comparison in this story. The significant comparison is WHY they stick with Harvard instead of transferring to a state college in which they could easily return to the elite ranks and realize their academic ambitions. The comparison is Harvard versus any of the roughly 5,300 other universities in the United States. These very bright children conclude it's better to go to Harvard and give up one's goals than to go anywhere else and achieve them. Is this conclusion an Opinion, a Value, or a Fact? In what category do you think the students regard and place this belief?

Comparison is a powerful belief fabricator that ultimately influences our self-identity, dreams, and decisions.

CHAPTER EXERCISE

If it's natural to compare and contrast, let's use it to our advantage in a thought experiment. Take a few moments to compare yourself (the person you are right now) with the person you will become if/when you accomplish your life goals and dreams.

What habits does the *successful you* have, that the *current you* doesn't?

What strengths of yours did the successful you maximize to get past the hurdles...and what weaknesses did they obviously overcome?

Does the successful you have greater certainty in your abilities? If so, which specific abilities? Those abilities are where you currently lack confidence, which are breeding grounds for limiting beliefs.

If they could mentor you, would the successful you advise you that your main obstacle is simply a fear of taking certain actions? Which actions? What makes you afraid?

Realize that **actions and time** are the only things separating the *current you* from the *successful you*. There are simply days of specific actions not yet executed. What are the top three belief differences between the current you and the successful you?

I would never die for my beliefs
because I might be wrong.

~ Bertrand Russell

CHAPTER 18

EMOTION

Let's imagine that your brilliance, your destiny, your ultimate success is being blocked by a Power Belief. And let's posit that whatever this Power Belief is in your head, it was not created by the usual suspects: direct experience, authority download, extrapolation, repetition, or comparison. Instead, let's pretend this Power Belief was created by a strong emotion.

Since this is a *limiting* Power Belief, we can suspect the emotion was negative in nature—fear, anger, jealousy, sadness, etc. Why? Because our minds pay much greater attention to negative (or potentially negative) stimuli than positive. Have you ever experienced a situation wherein many people were friendly or encouraging and yet you still remember that one S.O.B. who had something negative to say? Why is *negative* so powerful? We've evolved to generalize negativity (all hues

and degrees) as potential threats to our life and/or well-being. We pay more attention and give greater weight to scenarios, environments, people, and experiences that have embarrassed us, humiliated us, scared us, or physically hurt us. They're all negative in our book and imprint powerful engrams in our brain relating to the memory. From these engrams, powerful conclusions are formed. On the existential end of the spectrum, a rustling in the bushes, a dark path through the forest, or a mysterious car slowing down as it passes by, are all processed as potentially dangerous and life threatening. We form beliefs about these scenarios and ascribe them to the categories of either Values or Facts (mostly true/ nearly always true) even if the rustling turns out to be a stray cat, the forest path presented no monsters, and the car turned out to be a delivery driver slowing down to view addresses. Our belief that subsequent similar unknowns will still be threatening stays intact. On the shallow end of the spectrum, a snide comment, a rolling of the eyes, or a flippant dismissal of our beliefs are also processed as threats to our self-identity and thus our interpretation of reality. We immediately form conclusions about the offending person, scenario, or environment, and then file these away in our belief system where they serve our interests by either inspiring or inhibiting future behaviors.

In our catalog of emotionally derived beliefs, it is safe to assume there lives an innumerable population of limiting beliefs thwarting our desires and goals.

A humiliating experience during your third-grade solo cre-
ated a debilitating belief about performing before crowds or
placing yourself at the center of attention.

The death of a loved one caused you to stop believing in
God, and without God, Destiny seems like an arrogant fiction.

The heartbreak of unrequited love or the crushing jealousy
and rejection from an unfaithful partner have hardened you
from trusting others or ever exposing your true feelings.

Beliefs created and infused with strong emotions are
powerful. When working for you, you can become unde-
terred and unstoppable. When working against your interests, they are the proverbial anchor around your neck
weighing you down, punishing you more than helping you.

- SECTION SYNOPSIS -

Our belief systems are not a DNA-derived program giv-
en to us at birth. Our conclusions were adopted through
various progenitors. A demoralizing defeat early in life
that leads to the conclusion *"I am not good at (fill in the*
blank)"—may have been born of many mothers: Direct Experience, Emotion, Contrast...and if we witnessed a coach,
teacher, or parent shaking their head in disappointment,
we might also include Authority Download.

The reality is, most of our beliefs have the most un-
substantial evidence for their certainty, and yet we honor
them as we would Facts - *Nearly, Always True.* Sadly, some
people live and die and never pursue their wildest dreams
because of a single incident—or even a few—that caused

them embarrassment! Misinformed, ignorant, or off-the-cuff Opinions of **authority** figures were **downloaded** as truths into our developing minds, and there they stay to sabotage our goals and dreams. Often, when we **extrapolate**, we create conclusions while having absolutely zero **direct experience** with the conclusion. These faulty beliefs all mix and give us a very flawed understanding of reality.

However, we can learn a lot about how to reprogram our belief system by appreciating how it was programmed in the first place. Understand the six belief creation processes, and then use them to your advantage.

If previous authority figures programmed *doubt* in your abilities—find better, updated **authorities** who can see and convey the hidden assets you're not exploiting, and plant new conclusions. Don't use **contrast** to compare yourself with the *best* athletes, the *most successful* entrepreneurs, the *wealthiest and most famous* people...use it compare yourself with 6.75 billion *regular people* and recognize you're doing pretty damn good.

The strategy is not to replace limiting beliefs with false positives, but rather dilute the certainty of those limiting beliefs with empowering conclusions of equal or greater certainty.

POWER BELIEFS

THE PURPOSE, STRENGTHS, AND WEAKNESSES OF POWER BELIEFS

Know thy enemy
~ Sun Tzu

(22 & 35)

If you change the belief first,
changing the action is easier.

~ Peter McWilliams

CHAPTER 19

THE PABLO ESCOBAR STRATEGY

The title of this book is Power Beliefs, and culturally we are prone to automatically associate the term *power* with the word *force*. As a species, we generally find force repugnant, especially when it prevents us from getting our way. Therefore, any of your limiting Power Beliefs are most likely being assessed as an opponent, a thwarting nemesis to your life's goals and dreams. Because of our collective proclivity to view all opposition in a martial context, you are most likely expecting me to provide a martial solution to the obstacle of limiting Power Beliefs: eradicate, decimate, kill them, yank them like weeds! However, we are not looking for a psychic battle—we are simply looking for a win.

Let's suppose your grandfather told you as a child that your family doesn't produce rich people. This may be the originating cog in a cluster of limiting beliefs now preventing you from financial success. Your limiting Power Belief may be expressed as, *I'll never be wealthy*. Your grandfather's Authority Download can now easily be challenged and eliminated with what you've learned thus far which will help weaken the belief cluster supporting the limiting Power Belief. Although this one-by-one elimination process is feasible, it's what I would call that the Pablo Escobar strategy, and it's a long and protracted battle.

For those unfamiliar with Pablo Escobar, he was Columbia's most notorious drug cartel leader during the 1980s and 1990's. His wealth and power were so vast that he was effectively untouchable to legal prosecution. When the government eventually convicted him of illegal drug trade, assassinations, bombing, bribery, racketeering, and murder—Pablo basically agreed to voluntarily serve the sentence only if he was allowed to build and staff the "private prison" that would contain him. It was essentially a luxury home, guarded with his own cartel employees, helping him continue his drug operations from within.

Eventually, Pablo escaped his own prison. Those who sought to bring true justice to Pablo knew there was only one effective solution: assassination. However, Pablo was insulated and protected by his cartel soldiers and the thousands of government officials, police, military, and citizens on his payroll. Trying to locate him was nearly impossible as inside moles would inevitably tip him off. As you can imagine, not being able to find Pablo made it very difficult to kill Pablo. Therefore, a joint task force of Columbian military and U.S. DEA agents created a strategy whereby they would begin picking off his support network from the outermost circles first, and then work inward. In other words, kill off (or imprison) his network of supporters from least significant to most significant, hoping to eventually arrive at Pablo himself. If Pablo represented your limiting Power Belief—*I'll Never Be Wealthy*—they targeted Grandpa's original Authority Download, killed it, and then targeted the next minor limiting belief in the cluster. This systematic elimination continued as they worked their way upward toward the man in charge—the Power Belief itself. The strategy took a very long time, but in the end it worked. Pablo Escobar found himself without a support network and running for his life. He no longer had the ability to assemble meaningful resistance to the task force. On December 2, 1993, Pablo Escobar was shot and killed, proving even the untouchable can fall.

REFRAME THY ENEMY

I am not recommending the Pablo Escobar Strategy when it comes to neutralizing your limiting Power Beliefs. If all else fails, then maybe—BUT it is a very long process in trying to identify, let alone neutralize, all the members of a limiting cluster. No person truly knows how many conclusions they have surrounding any meaningful topic. Succeeding in doing so is also bound to have unintended, secondary repercussions to your psyche. Some of those beliefs you neutralized might have served your happiness in other clusters. We do not want to hit your belief system with napalm. We need to be strategic and holistic in our approach.

In the following chapters you'll learn about REFRAMING, which is the magic weapon in your fight against limiting beliefs of all varieties. Reframing simply means seeing something from a new perspective or in a different light. For instance, *vanity* is often considered a personality flaw. It's loosely defined as excessive pride in one's self. Somewhere in history man determined it's bad to have excessive pride in one's self. But we could also see vanity as a gift that allows someone to keep trying when a goal hasn't been accomplished or to keep trying when others tell them it can't be done. Vanity may have helped break the four-minute mile which freed all mankind from a limiting Power Belief. National vanity motivated us to lift off the planet, travel to the moon, and establish satellites that today improve the life of nearly everyone on earth. Vanity may be a hidden motivator in a future cure for cancer. Learning how to reframe is necessary and is the fastest and most holistic tactic to changing the beliefs that limit your life.

In the upcoming chapters, I will reframe the idea of *belief warfare* through various analogies and metaphors to help you better understand your opponent and to demonstrate the art of reframing. In *knowing thy enemy,* you'll eventually come to see **a limiting Power Belief not as a virus trying to hurt you, but as an outdated vaccine still trying to save you.** I'll also introduce a strategic process by which you can effectively change any limiting belief for the rest of your life.

CHAPTER 20

NEVER SURRENDER

On Sunday, September 2, 1945, World War II came to its official end at 9:09 a.m. when General Douglas MacArthur formally accepted Imperial Japan's official surrender. I repeat and emphasize: *official* surrender, *official* end.

Preceding this momentous event, 250 days earlier, on December 26, 1944, a Japanese intelligence officer by the name of Hiroo Onoda was sent to Lubang Island in the Philippines to help thwart the Ally advance. Should the allies capture the island, they would have a viable base with which to attack the Japanese homeland with long-range bombers. This would be very bad news for Japan.

Onoda's orders were clear—he was to do everything possible to prevent an American take-over of the island which included destroying infrastructure such as an airstrip and harbor pier. To successfully carry out his mission, Onoda, a Second Lieutenant, was also commanded to never surrender and never take his own life. At 22 years old, death or victory were the only acceptable outcomes available to this patriotic young man.

For reasons unclear, upon arriving on the island, Japanese officers outranking Onoda prevented the destruction of the airstrip and pier which eventually helped the American and Philippine forces recapture Lubang in early March 1945. The Japanese resistance on Lubang was routed. Imperial soldiers either surrendered or were killed in battle. Onoda and three of his fellow fighters survived the fray and fled to the jungles where they continued to do everything possible to thwart the allies. 186 days later, World War II came to an end. Its official end. At least for the rest of the planet.

Meanwhile, in the jungles...

Onoda, having the highest rank of the four soldiers, takes command of his small guerilla squad and continues to engage with Philippine police for literally years... more specifically, decades. Yes, Onoda and his men refuse to accept incoming news about the war being over. They wrongfully conclude such information is merely propaganda trying to lure them out from hiding. The first rumors reach them in October 1945 when they find a leaflet explaining the war has ended. As that year draws to a close, more leaflets are dropped by plane, but this time from the Japanese General of their Fourteenth Army ordering them to surrender. The leaflets are again interpreted as Ally propaganda. Seven years later, in 1952, letters and family pictures are dropped from aircraft, once more urging the soldiers to surrender. Of the four soldiers, one eventually does surrender in 1950, two die from skirmishes with Philippine patrols, and only Second Lieutenant Hiroo Onoda is left keeping the Japanese war machine alive.

In early 1974, Onoda is found by a Japanese "hippie boy" named Norio Suzuki who has flown to the island specifically to search for the fabled soldier. When asked by Suzuki why he will not come out and surrender, Onoda relays that he is awaiting direct orders from his superiors. Suzuki returns to Japan to help make this happen. On February 20, 1974, Onoda's mission ends when he is officially relieved of duty by his commanding officer. No longer an active soldier, he peacefully surrenders to the Philippine government.

Hiroo Onoda is undoubtedly the greatest personification of a Power Belief I could hope to find. Unstoppable commitment to his Duty is perhaps the best understanding of this soldier who, for 30 years, refused to surrender when it must have seemed in his own best interests to do so.

We will never know the intensity or number of Power Beliefs that held Onoda so steadfast to his mission. Hiroo Onoda's lost opportunities for joy, family, career, and peace were replaced by a vigilance to duty he could not accept as having crossed a realistic expiration date. All signs of the war being over were simply interpreted as deceitful propaganda.

Like all Power Beliefs, Onoda believed he served and defended something greater than just himself. I'm sure he truly believed he was still protecting Japan even with so many convincing indications the war was over. I'm sure there were months, if not years, of self-torment, glimpsing a more peaceful and enjoyable life if he just surrendered his jungle post. Even upon believing the war had ended, Onoda refused to yield, until his higher-ranking Commanding Officer (think, *category hierarchy*) first honored and then decommissioned his service.

The history books will show that Onoda was never defeated. He was never beaten into submission. Pledged to a life of warfare, it's ironic that violence and force were not the remedy to his predicament. The same is true for our limiting Power Beliefs. You cannot think of them as an enemy that must be destroyed and killed. Attacking them only convinces them to dig in deeper. Power Beliefs have an unstoppable commitment to their duty and will only surrender upon being decommissioned from a higher certainty ensuring that safety and the greater good will prevail. They must be honored for their service no matter how much joy and happiness they have unwittingly prevented. They are, after all, simply doing the job they were programmed to do.

CHAPTER TAKE-AWAY

Limiting Power Beliefs are a natural part of us, not an outside parasite that must be exterminated. As such, whenever we seek to get rid of these committed soldiers, we need to take into account they have been given specific orders to defend us without surrender or suicide. They were originally programmed to protect us from real or imagined physical or egoic harm—and they are "true believers" in their cause—defending us, preventing humiliation, scorn, and destruction upon our life. Only in finding their whereabouts, understanding their mission, and issuing orders from a higher command, can they be convinced to step out of the jungle and retire, peacefully.

We know your limiting Power Beliefs are hiding within your subconscious mind. Our conscious mission is to now find them, determine what category they are operating from, and then use higher belief levels to decommission them. If they are serving the highest levels (Alphas and Truths) we'll use beliefs from the same hierarchy to reframe them. This is how we maintain a holistic approach toward your programming.

Understand that any limiting belief that is blocking you is doing so because at some point in your past, there was more safety in remaining put than in marching you forward. Regardless of how this belief entered your mind (Direct Experience, Authority Download, Extrapolation, etc) you adopted it with certainty. When you feel fear about taking actions, extending outside your comfort zone, it's because you **doubt** achieving the success that lives down that pathway. Your mind will always favor certainty, even if it costs you your dreams.

Our battle plan is to instill certainty.

When someone is delusional, he or she can do
anything to justify his or her beliefs.

~ Debasish Mridha

CHAPTER 21

THE FORCE FIELD

To change Power Beliefs, you first need to understand Rule #1: *Power Beliefs DO NOT want to be changed!*

Power Beliefs are uniquely protected to prevent change from happening on their watch. Like commanding officers standing behind tight battle formations, they are both insulated from direct exposure and view contrary beliefs as dire threats to the entire stabilized (belief) system. They are surrounded by bodyguards, frontlines, and columns of clustered beliefs forming a quasi-impenetrable fortress within the mind. This fort prevents contrary beliefs from planting their invading, foreign flags!

As this may sound like a fanciful analogy of how your mind works, let's explore a *theory of mind* that will help explain all this in the simplest way possible.

THEORY OF MIND

Let's start with the day you were born. Your mind was basically empty. Like an empty circle. Outside of instincts, you had very little knowledge about the world, and there were few if

any conclusions programmed into your consciousness. But soon the stimuli, inputs, and data started pouring in like water over Niagara Falls.

In the early years of life, from birth to about the age of seven, humans operate within a low frequency brain wave known as Theta. This frequency is highly receptive. What  does that mean? It means it takes in EVERYTHING! Children are basically sponges, absorbing everything—all the information coming at them—all the conclusions, stories, authority downloads—they are just receiving and accepting it. They have not yet developed the ability to analyze it consciously to evaluate and reject any of it. That is why children believe in Santa Claus, giant bunnies delivering candy, tooth fairies, unicorns, magic, and all the other fantasies presented to their theta receptivity.

Along with the possibility of animals being able to talk and monsters being real, children also take in all the assessments (Authority Downloads) told to them by parents, teachers and older siblings. Comments such as:

You're stupid
You're ugly
You're a bad boy/girl
You're such a disappointment
Why can't you do anything right?

All these statements go straight into the child's head as truthful conclusions. They eventually learn (through pattern recognition) that certain people change their voices to tease and joke, and so some information is understood as purposeful silliness, but most everything else is simply accepted as Truth.

An amazing thing happens between the ages of six and eight when the child's mind has filled with enough knowledge, enough understanding about reality, that they are now able to process incoming stimuli against that which they already know. In so doing, they begin to critically evaluate incoming information as true or false. The mind has reached a tipping point where it now has enough conclusions coded into its database that it begins to create a filter, similar to anti-virus software, to identify and reject nonsense and harmful beliefs from infecting the overall platform.

You will notice during these ages that children will start asking smarter questions. The information inside their heads starts re-evaluating inputs such as Santa Claus. They contrast the flying reindeer claim against *other animals that can fly* and find a shocking discrepancy—only birds fly. Flying reindeer don't fit any pattern recognition, or

any direct experience. *Note to 8 year old self: Flying reindeer sounds like BS!*

This process continues for the rest of our lives. Our minds simply cross-reference our database to find beliefs that vouch for other beliefs. The mind analyzes conflicting beliefs to determine which is more certain, discards the loser, and then assigns the *accepted* conclusions to their appropriate hierarchical categories. This happens day in and day out. With every conversation, with each exposure to new information, the scrutiny continues. This is the ever-evolving formation of your *critical filter.*

YOUR CRITICAL FILTER

The beliefs you've accepted now act as a gatekeeper—filtering all incoming information. You can think of them

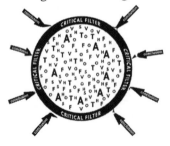

as a filter or even more so like a Grand Jury. When a new belief is presented to your mind (e.g. flying saucers are real) this belief is cross-referenced with your existing beliefs (members of the grand jury) and is evaluated to determine its credibility. If the new belief doesn't jibe with your current beliefs, it is summarily rejected.

These grand juries are comprised of like-minded, closely-knit bureaucrats with a Power Belief presiding over the hearing. These juries hold sway not only over our belief system, but our actions, too.

Devastating Power Beliefs come to power when faulty conclusions find themselves embedded into the programming *before* the critical filter matures. A child who is told *you are a loser, you are fat and ugly and dumb, you'll never amount to anything,* accepts such conclusions as truths.

Depending on the frequency of hearing such statements and how many people may have said such terrible things, those beliefs were reinforced within the child's mind, with few (if any)  counterclaims being offered for download. As they aged, all contradictory evidence of these conclusions first had to get past the grand jury whose job it was to uphold the validity that they are in fact a loser, fat, ugly or dumb, or that they'll never amount to anything. If your critical filter *locked in* faulty, limiting beliefs, your grand jury will inevitably reject proof and testimony that you're a winner, a beautiful person, someone bound for success. Have you ever met someone who totally rejects compliments? Someone who corrects you when you say something positive about them? Most likely they have pernicious beliefs trapped inside their critical filter and they're not going to let your conclusions in, even if they want to. Your critical filter is the force field we first need to penetrate before we can capture and reframe any limiting Power Beliefs. Penetrating your critical filter, however, is difficult.

In the next chapter we'll explore how your critical filter is able to *warp reality* to prevent conflicting conclusions a seat at the table.

CHAPTER 22

WARPING REALITY

As humans, we tend to affiliate with people most like ourselves. We prefer to affiliate with members of our own gender, age, race, religion, political party, and social status more so than with those outside our personal demographics and worldview. Having others echo back our reality gives us certainty...and **certainty is an addictive drug on which our minds are hooked.**

In fact, we frequently warp reality in order to get our needed fix—our daily doses of certainty. Yes, I did say *warp reality,* and unfortunately this is not a metaphor. We censor, distort, and delete most perceptions of the external world which do not corroborate our inner belief system. This warping is known as **Confirmation Bias** and it's time to introduce three of the top illusionists supplying us with our pseudo-certainty. Each illusionist alters reality so we can continue to experience a world most in-line with our programmed belief system.

The first is **Selective Exposure**. Selective exposure is the tendency for an individual to expose themselves to information, people, scenarios, and events that reinforce their pre-existing beliefs while simultaneously avoiding competing or contradictory ones.

Selective exposure is why you frequent the same restaurants, why hip-hop fans don't go to country concerts, why half the country tunes in to conservative news and the

other half prefers the liberal media. It's why you don't openly embrace different religions, political ideas, ethnic customs, or opposing philosophies. You simply do not allow yourself to be *exposed* to these differing beliefs. Why? Because they don't harmonize with your critical filter.

Certainty Illusionist:
SELECTIVE EXPOSURE

White Supremacists don't go to NAACP meetings and minorities don't attend Klan rallies. Fans of Nascar don't frequent the opera, and opera fans aren't usually at Wrestle-Mania events. Humans expose themselves to that which they know, understand, agree with—and thus *enjoy*. By restricting our exposure to that which we already agree with, we reinforce our conclusions and strengthen the critical filter that protects our belief system.

Selective Exposure isn't inherently good or bad for a person. A person who is happy, well-adjusted, productive and realizing their potential may benefit themselves by staying on course and not allowing outside information to derail them. However, there's always the risk that your self-regulated reality will stunt your potential because the elements necessary to grow your life may never be introduced or discovered.

The second illusionist we employ to reinforce our certainty is called **Selective Perception.** This is when an individual processes information to make it fit with their beliefs—even if it objectively doesn't. It's basically mental manipulation. A self-imposed, automated reframe of reality.

Certainty Illusionist:
SELECTIVE PERCEPTION

Here's how it works:

Let's say I really dislike politicians. I believe they are the most self-serving, dishonest, power-grabbing, phonies on the planet.

And let's say, quite by accident, I happen across some information that presents one of these cretins in a very favorable light—very decent, kind, and generous. Maybe they did something that really improved the life of someone who needed it, or maybe they significantly helped a worthy cause or community.

This information must now be processed by my critical filter, which is packed with belief clusters refuting the possibility of any politician being a decent human. Having seen it, heard it, directly experienced it—I was ultimately exposed to something that didn't match my beliefs. So, what happens now? Well it's really simple... I just reframe the perception. I conclude this politician did it for publicity or some other self-serving need—and presto, whamo—my beliefs, certainty, and reality are once again reinforced. Stability returns to the system. Everything is back to normal. And Selective Perception isn't just wielded to *indict* politicians. It is able to *exonerate* them as well. It allows us to explain away all the obvious lies, manipulations, and corruption committed by politicians on our side of the aisle, justifying their actions by ascribing some nuanced technicality or vast conspiracy against them. Does any of this seem familiar?

Selective Perception is used by religions against religions, politicians against politicians, and ethnicities against ethnicities all the time. One simply comes up with believable excuses to make reality once again resonate with our critical filter. Instead of questioning our filter, we simply reframe the experience so it resonates and produces certainty again.

Selective Perception is not inherently bad or good. Successful people, especially entrepreneurs, have an amazing ability to interpret failures as merely *learning opportunities.* As a matter of fact, if you cultivated your belief system so your critical filter diluted any incoming evidence of failure, if you could commission Power Beliefs to summarily reject any conclusions suggesting you are not destined for greatness—it's highly likely you'd end up being a powerful Titan in your field of interest. If your critical filter can repel conclusions (which it does anyway), why not have it repel those conclusions that obstruct your goals and dreams?

The third illusionist we use to warp reality is called **Selective Retention**, which simply means we give preference

to memories of events and experiences that match our belief system while repressing those that don't.

When a person believes themselves dumb, or bad at
public speaking, or unlovable, they can often recall example after example of instances where this was proven true.
They can easily remember failing that test, or mumbling
their words in that one sentence, or
how many times their love was unrequited. Most likely they also experienced times when they did well in
school, spoke eloquently, and were
loved by others...but only memories
that confirm the negative conclusions
are retained for quick access. The
others are forgotten.

Certainty Illusionist:
SELECTIVE RETENTION

This works for positive memories as well. Great athletes
will retain victories and use these to fortify belief in their
abilities, discarding and forgetting all the times they failed.

All three warping techniques are used for the purpose
of confirmation bias, which serves to feed a steady loop of
certainty back into the system.

But in case I've presented your mind as some impen-
etrable Fort Knox, guarded with retinal scans, double-
agents, and duplicitous mind-altering supervillains, I'd like
to reframe once again. Yes, your beliefs *are* loyal and dis-
criminating and eager to malign and banish any interloper
that doesn't conform. But your mind is less like a *CIA meets*

X-men movie plot and more like the political machinations of your average middle school.

CHAPTER TAKE-AWAY

To preserve the certainty, you have in your current belief system, you allow your mind to distort incoming information to confirm what you already believe. This is widely known as Confirmation Bias. In essence, you are remaining inside a belief system bubble and mentally manipulate reality so as not to burst this bubble.

The following three illusionists are the genies that can make all your dreams come true or imprison you in your bubble .

SELECTIVE EXPOSURE

This illusionist prefers you only expose yourself to information and experiences consistent with your current conclusions.

SELECTIVE PERCEPTION

This illusionist alters your perception of conflicting information or events to conform with what you already believe.

SELECTIVE RETENTION

This illusionist conveniently causes you to remember experiences that confirm your beliefs and forget those that contradict them.

CHAPTER 23

THE COOL CLIQUE

Now you can take this with a grain of salt, but Power Beliefs are also similar to those proverbial cool cliques in junior high schools; popular, powerful, and seemingly insurmountable. They're never swayed by protests or appeals from underlings. They are loaded with attitude, and they hold absolute power over who is permitted to join their stratosphere. The Power Beliefs (cool kids) can be mean and abusive, but oddly they derive this power only through the compliance of the entire belief system (student body). Sure, it's often a dysfunctional arrangement, but it's also a stabilized system. Since our minds like nothing more than predictability (certainty), the cool kids get to rule the roost!

RIDICULOUS CATEGORICAL HIERARCHY ANALOGY
Alphas......................Popular Kids
Truths......................Athletes & Cheerleaders
Facts........................Class Clowns & Talented Kids
Values......................Gossipy Brown Nosers

Superstitions.........Goths & Emos
Hopes....................Ugly Ducklings & Awkward Geniuses

Within each school there exists a naturally formed pecking order. The same is true of your belief system. Each subsequent category of the pecking order has a lesser degree of influence upon the overall system, and it's usually quite tough to move up the ladder once you've been categorized. It's not impossible, just very difficult.

It might be tempting given the junior high analogy to identify limiting Power Beliefs as the Bullies of the school, and this fits to a degree. Bullies do create unnecessary stress and tension, thwarting and blocking the desired experience of so many outside their own circle of friends. In this manner, they do act like limiting Power Beliefs. After that, however, the analogy disappears. Real-life bullies never justify their actions as necessary to the holistic well-being of the student body. When a bully beats up Malcolm and destroys his award-winning science project, he doesn't do so to make the school safer. *Unless Malcolm finally figured out that black hole ray gun he and Eugene were discussing!* No, a bully intimidates and thwarts for the psychological pleasure of domination. It's simply a more public form of self-gratification. A Power Belief is different. It's actually convinced it is serving the greater good by keeping potentially harmful beliefs from upsetting the belief system, which in this case, stabilizes your life.

When I contemplate quitting my job and pursing my dream, a limiting Power Belief steps in to say, *Whoa! What if you fail? And here are all the ways you can fail big. And here's all the bad stuff that's going to happen because you quit your job and pursued this!!!*

The limiting Power Belief considers itself the voice of reason, backed by clusters of other conclusions within your belief system. If you were to ask a limiting Power Belief which character it most corresponds with in our junior high analogy, it might say, the educators, the counselors, the school nurse, and the principal—all rolled into one! Its job is to run and control the school, and sometimes that requires tough love and discipline. If you were to suggest to real-life educators, counselors, nurses, and principals, that they just chill, step aside, and let the kids do whatever they want, and even allow unregistered kids to enter the building and mix among the classrooms, they would act like limiting Power Beliefs and also reject and sabotage such an idea. Terrible consequences could ensue.

Limiting Power Beliefs are simply preventing that proverbial *out-of-control cafeteria food fight on spaghetti day* from breaking out inside your mind. Or from the whole school laughing at you. Usually both.

Unfortunately, they haven't realized you've already graduated.

The power of our beliefs can work in either
direction to become life affirming or life denying.

~ Gregg Braden

CHAPTER 24

COUPLES THERAPY

For one final reframe of your belief system, let's pretend you and your limiting belief are at an impasse over the direction of your career. Your dream is to start your own business. The Power Belief is preventing you from trying.

LIMITING POWER BELIEF
You shouldn't start your own business.
You can't. You're too old, inexperienced, and unreliable.

YOUR DREAM
Why do you have to be so negative?
This is my destiny!

LIMITING POWER BELIEF
Look, I'm clustered with a lot of other conclusions that support me on this.
First of all, there's the Fact you've never started a business before. Ever! Which leads me to conclude you pulling off a start-up is an Opinion at best or Hope at the least; both are very low in certainty.
(continued)

LIMITING POWER BELIEF (Cont'd)
There's also a ton of Authority Downloads
I speak with daily—*all Facts by the way,
which means higher certainty*—about the
high percentage of start-up failures.

YOUR DREAM
How can I provide pattern recognition
certainty to prove I can run a business, if
you never let me start a business in the
first place?

LIMITING POWER BELIEF
That's a good point, I'll admit. But what
if you're wrong? For a minute, let's consider
if you failed. Your self-identity... you've
been working on that your whole life...
now you're gonna just roll the dice and
risk it?

YOUR DREAM
I want my self-identity to also include
being an entrepreneur.

LIMITING POWER BELIEF
Then you should have thought of that
before. You should have gone to business
school! You are not the only belief that
fails should this venture fail. Self-esteem
and confidence will plummet.

YOUR DREAM
And they'll rise if I succeed-

LIMITING POWER BELIEF
The operative word being IF – *if you succeed*. When your inexperience,which is also a Fact, meets with reality, and should there be a crash... because statistical Facts are telling me it's a long shot for first-time start-ups to succeed, so a crash is highly likely—and when that happens, unknown consequences will ensue. Unt-uh! No accidents! No unknown consequences! My sole job is to protect you financially, reputationally, emotionally... and with the ledger book as I see it, I have less certainty in your eventual success, than I do in your eventual failure. Discussion over. I won't support this.

The mind craves certainty. It is addicted to certainty. It abhors unexpected and/or undesirable change. Being a certainty addict, it will sell you out to get its fix regarding any important issue. The limiting Power Belief is simply trying to protect you financially or uphold your reputation should you fail.

- SECTION SYNOPSIS -

- The #1 Rule Of Power Beliefs is they do not want to be changed.

- Power Beliefs resist change for two main reasons:

  ▸ They were programmed early in life, before our belief system matured, so they are now *locked inside* our critical filter, imbued with high certainty.

  ▸ They were originally programmed to protect us from real or imagined physical, emotional, or egoic harm. They are "true believers" in their cause, defending us by preventing possible humiliation, scorn, and destruction upon our life.

- When contradictory conclusions are presented to our belief system they are summarily rejected, either through outright dismissal, or through mental manipulation (warping reality) to make them appear as confirming our beliefs.

- To reprogram Limiting Power Beliefs, we need to get past the critical filter, utilize current beliefs from higher categories, and reframe so as to preserve the integrity and holistic nature of the belief system.

- Limiting Power Beliefs should not be viewed as viruses that need to be killed, but rather outdated vaccines that once helped us, but are no longer needed.

POWER BELIEFS

HOW TO REPROGRAM YOUR BELIEF SYSTEM

Live your beliefs and you can turn the world around.

~ Henry David Thoreau

CHAPTER 25

THE SCALES OF REALITY

The function of your mind is to create coherence between your programming and your reality.
~ Dr. Bruce Lipton

Well here we are...you basically know more about the nuts and bolts of Beliefs than the vast majority of the world. You endured the previous pages because you wanted to know if a single Power Belief can either deliver your dreams or block them. This final section will focus on both instances. We not only want to neutralize your limiting Power Beliefs, but we want to replace them with conclusions that will drive you forward. Firing one manager without replacing him is bad for business.

WHY CHANGING YOUR BELIEFS WILL WORK

Your mind acts like a scale, always trying to balance whatever you believe with what you experience as reality.

As discussed in Chapter 22, the mind does everything it can to make the two sides balance. It warps, censors, and distorts your reality to keep equilibrium between your internal and external worlds. It does this because it craves certainty and stability!

The mind values its own integrity over external reality. It blocks opposing conclusions with its critical filter and is the sole arbiter of conflicts between what it believes and what it experiences.

WHEN REALITY CAN'T BE BLOCKED

Have you ever heard stories of an overweight person who loses considerable weight, seems happier and healthier, get heaps of compliments and praise from their family and friends, but ultimately regains the original weight, or even more? It's sometimes said even though the person is *thin on the outside*, they are still *fat on the inside*, and so the mind must manipulate reality to make the outer balance with the inner.

How about accounts of common people winning millions of dollars in lottery jackpots only to be broke again in a span of a couple years? It's said they have a poor mindset. They identify with being poor (or not being rich) from a lifetime of experience (direct experience, repetition), and so their mind sabotages the outer reality to once again find balance with the inner.

In both examples, external reality confronts the mind with real, measurable, undeniable discrepancies to its internal programming. The mind, being as powerful as it is, simply begins to do everything it can to stabilize the system, which includes enacting behaviors and additional beliefs that will bring things back to normal. Back to balance. It regains  the weight and it loses the money. *There, everything is normal again. You're welcome!* The mind does not want a great body or money; it wants stability and certainty. It thinks it's doing you a favor.

Changing one's external reality without first changing the internal belief system disrupts both certainty and stability and sends the mind reeling into action to restore both.

THE SUBCONSCIOUS MIND ALWAYS WINS

The central premise of this book is that all enduring change first comes from reprogramming one's belief system which aligns your internal reality with your desired external reality. Upon changing your beliefs, external discrepancies now confuse and irritate the mind which again, values its integrity foremost. The mind, doing what it does best, attempts to once again create equilibrium between its programming and external reality. It begins enacting behaviors and leveraging additional beliefs to make reality bend to its conclusions. **It now.makes the outer balance with the inner!**

So, if I just believe I'm a millionaire, my mind will make it so? Well, yes...and no. Just believing and thinking the universe is going to fill your bank account may align with everyone's Hopes, but we have many more conclusions that let us know this isn't how reality works. Changing beliefs allows for the manifestation of new actions and different

behaviors. These new actions and behaviors are the source to realizing the money. Doing what you've always done, will produce what you've always had. Doing new things changes your life. Truly believing you're a millionaire should create dissatisfaction with your current reality. It should inspire and drive you to learn what needs to be learned, to become valuable in an area that gets rewarded with money. Millionaires are not wealthy because they have money. Millionaires are wealthy because of how they think and what they do. The poor lottery winner who goes bust proves this point. Legitimate millionaires think differently, and they think differently because they have different conclusions about work, sacrifice, commitment, opportunity, and self-identity than do their counterparts, the average Joe and Jane. This thinking produces the money. And should they go broke, they can simply earn it back again. Their minds are programmed to manifest their millionaire reality. The subconscious mind always wins.

So yes, to come back around—it starts with believing! Your goal from this day forward should be to reprogram your belief system, to create an imbalance between your internal conclusions and your external reality. But it must be an imbalance toward your dream and for your mind's benefit. Critical to your success is eliminating any Power Beliefs that stand in your way.

HOW TO DISCOVER LIMITING POWER BELIEFS

We need to start at the end and work backwards by identifying the core goal or dream you truly desire.

There are two components to your goals we will need to investigate. The first is the finalized attainment of the goal itself. *What is the essence of the literal goal?* The second is the Action Plan (behaviors and activities) that will deliver this dream. *What needs to be done to attain the goal?*

Since nearly everybody would like to be wealthier (for various reasons) I have chosen to demonstrate the process of identifying, reframing, and supplanting Power Beliefs by creating an example goal based on wealth. I hope that in choosing this tract it will have the broadest application for readers. This is to demonstrate how the process works. The steps presented can work for any dream or goal.

So, let's begin by positing a very popular life ambition—**becoming a millionaire.** Now, if you're already a millionaire, perhaps you want to bump that up to a becoming a decamillionaire—or billionaire.

THE BASIS OF GOALS AND DREAMS

Worthy Digression: It has been my lifelong experience that **all our dreams and goals are in service of a desire to feel happy.** What does that mean? It simply means what we think we want isn't what we *really* want. What we really want is to be happy. We conclude achieving the goal will deliver this happiness. Goals and dreams are themselves a means to an end. We think we want to lose weight when what we really want is to be happy. Losing weight is how we think we'll achieve happiness.

I want to travel the world. Why? Because I think that will make me happy. I want to own my own restaurant and become a millionaire. Why? Because I think that will make me happy. I want to be a famous (fill in the blank). Why? I think you get the idea.

I can go on and on with examples, but the purpose of bringing this up now is for you to get very clear about what it is you truly want and whether or not your dream will actually deliver it. Will it take you further away (physically and/or emotionally) from family and friends? Will it force you to abandon lesser activities and habits that already make you happy?

It is a futile waste of your life energy to reprogram your belief system, put in the time and effort of executing the behaviors and activities needed to accomplish your goals, only to cross the finish line without your true prize— Happiness!

That being said, I also have high certainty that humans feel happy when they feel successful. And the greatest definition of success I have ever come across is, *one's steady progress toward the attainment of worthwhile goals.* Success and happiness are not reserved for that single moment when you cross the finish line. You'll feel them with each step forward—as you inch closer and closer to worthwhile goals. These moments of success and happiness, based on progress alone, are indications the goal is right for you. If you do not experience happiness along the journey, I'd advise you to re-evaluate that in which you're investing your life. As I stated on page one, the greatest tragedy is for us to die with so much *what-could-have-been* still trapped inside us. Do not waste your life pursuing generic dreams whose finish lines are merely money, prestige, fame, or status. Multitudes who have attained these goals have warned us—*these things in themselves **do not** bring happiness.*

Go for your dreams...but first let your heart determine the destination. Then use your mind to drive you there.

All personal breakthroughs begin
with a change in beliefs.

~ Anthony Robbins

CHAPTER 26

STEP 1

EVALUATING THE EMOTIONAL CERTAINTY YOU HAVE IN ACCOMPLISHING YOUR DREAM

THE FIRST PROBLEM YOU MAY FACE: *Doubt*. Often life goals are too daunting and thus unbelievable. The attainment is simply beyond your most reasonable levels of certainty.

Example Dream: *I want to be a millionaire.*

Current Reality: *I make $55,000 per year. I have about $15,000 in investments and roughly $3,000 in liquid savings. Furthermore, I'm a teacher with little opportunity to earn more money.*

Running this goal through an initial sniff test, it's bound to be returned with a certainty level of **Hope**. Possibly **Opinion**. To fully succeed, we need to have our goal and dream at least at the level of **Values**. The higher up the certainty level, the better.

Now there are many success coaches and new age gurus who will preach, *just fake it till ya make it*, meaning just pretend you are already a millionaire. You're just waiting for it to manifest. That alone, *with nothing else*, will guarantee failure and have you doubt that any of this belief stuff works.

In our current example, the mind will most likely reject certainty in this goal. Why? The gap is too wide, the teacher doesn't have an Action Plan on how to earn the money, and external reality is screaming *Not A Millionaire!*

My claim is that your first obstacle will most likely be DOUBT. That does not mean it's insurmountable, but to overcome the mind's doubt we need to maximize certainty to levels above Hope, Superstition, and Opinion. This is merely Step 1, which indicates there are multiple steps to get you there. We are simply discussing what you should do if there's greater doubt than certainty.

Your best option is to bridge the gap between the $55,000 and one million dollars is to find certainty at least at the level of Values (Mostly True). Find an amount that stretches you just beyond your comfort zone, but which you have high certainty is attainable.

Example: *Becoming a millionaire is a stretch, but it's way more possible for me to make $100,000...on my way to becoming a millionaire.*

If your dream is to become a millionaire, but you just don't believe it due to your current financial situation, but you **do** believe you could achieve $100,000, then by all means set your sites on $100,000. After all, you cannot have a million dollars without also having $100,000. Let the hundred thousand dollars be the starting point—your reasonable bridge to one million.

THE SECOND PROBLEM YOU MAY FACE: *Indifference.*

The goal is too small and unmotivating. There's no emotional excitement!

Regarding lifestyles, products, and habits, humans do not swap that which is considered *good enough* for something promised to be *slightly better*. This is something marketers, advertisers, and salespeople fail to understand. Slightly better does not evoke *any* powerful emotions. It doesn't inspire us to act.

All things being equal:

We don't change our auto insurance to save $50 a year, unless we believe $4.16 per month surpasses slightly better.

We don't leave our current mobile carrier simply for the benefit of not being locked into a contract.

We don't change jobs for an extra $1 per hour, unless, that $1 per hour is greater than slightly better.

So it is with our goals and dreams as well. A *slightly better life* would never be called a *dream*. We are motivated by greater gains.

To motivate humans, there needs to be a change (or experience) that will makes us feel markedly better about our reality.

Remember, **happiness** is the *why*—the **goal/dream** is simply the *how*.

Sometimes our dream is just too small to get excited about, and without excitement (or other positive emotions) we're not going to follow through on what needs to be done to achieve it. Sure, the purpose of creating a small goal may have been founded on great intentions (practicality, modesty, probability) but as human beings, we seldom, if ever, trade good enough for slightly better. So, it's better to elevate your goals and expectations to a level that inspires you and fills you with excitement, optimism, and joy.

If you want to be a millionaire but doubt that can happen, lower your goal. If lowering your goal to $100,000 is uninspiring, my advice is to keep bumping the goal upward until it's both exciting *and* possesses a high degree of certainty. In our scenario, let's pretend you settle on $250,000. That amount is both exciting *and* you have relatively high certainty it can be achieved.

$250,000 now becomes the Dream we need to program our belief system toward. We will eventually do two things:

Reframe any limiting Power Belief currently preventing the realization of this goal .

Program a new Power Belief that drives you toward the goal .

The purpose of STEP 1 is to gauge your emotional certainty and excitement. Reprogramming your mind with low-certainty beliefs won't work because the mind will simply assign such beliefs into their acknowledged low-certainty categories—most likely **Hope.** You will not have changed any programming.

Also, having high certainty with low excitement won't result in accomplishing your goals if the timeframe is of any moderate length. Sticking with something for weeks, months, or years only happens with positive emotional fuel driving your activities. This too can be managed, but if raging excitement is not there in the beginning, you need to ask yourself, WHY do you even want this goal?

If I have the belief that I can do it, I shall surely
acquire the capacity to do it even if I may not
have it at the beginning.

~ Gandhi

CHAPTER 27

STEP 2

FILTER YOUR DREAM THROUGH YOUR ALPHAS/VALUES FOR OBJECTIONS

The next step is to test your dream against beliefs within your Alpha category. Remember your Alpha category contains your beliefs about the ultimate cosmic Truths. *Why we're here - what's our purpose?* Such Alphas eventually find external expression in our **Values,** which relay how we should behave toward life, the planet, and other sentient beings. Values tell what actions and thoughts represent our highest self. These are our highest existential beliefs. These beliefs help inform us if we're a good person or not. Most limiting beliefs which can be dealt with reside in a quasi-blend of Alpha and Value beliefs. We need to get these categories to *bless our dreams,* so to speak.

Here are Four Practical Considerations when filtering any dream through your Alpha-Value Beliefs. We'll explore each one using our $250,000 Goal to exemplify how each can produce a limiting Power Belief.

Will any of these violate your Higher Beliefs?

1. *The literal result of attaining your dream*

2. *The Intention or desire behind wanting the dream*

3. *What achieving the dream might then lead to*

4. *What others you care about might think of you if you attain the dream. Will they judge you as a bad character?*

1. The literal attainment of your dream

In what ways does attaining the literal goal put you at odds with your highest self? For instance, in our example of $250,000, would making that money be contrary to the *best possible YOU?* If modesty and humility are your highest Values, that sum may create discomfort and be an objectionable endeavor. If so, your subconscious will kill it and make sure it never manifests.

2. The background intentions for wanting the dream

What is the real reason you want the money? Is it because you want to seem important? Do you want to boost your ego and prove you're successful? Are you wanting money to buy things and show off? Or are you needing it to send your kids to college or to help your aging parents? Besides the literal paper money, what else do you stand to gain? For millions of people, the stigmas of greed and

- YOUR WORKBOOK -
Filtering Dream Though Alpha-Values

List Your Dream/Goal:

1. In what ways does attaining the literal goal put you at odds with your highest self?

Possible Objections:

2. What is the real reason you want the dream?

Possible Objections:

selfishness are often associated with wealth. Greed and selfishness often run contrary to Alpha-Values. Your highest self cannot be greedy and selfish. (Or so historical programming suggests.) Our intentions are central to our character. If we want that money to buy a boat or other materials goods and our Alpha-Values think that's egotistical—our subconscious is going to ensure it never happens.

3. What might this lead to?

What is bound to happen after you attain the goal? Could gaining significantly more money possibly make you materialistic or compromise your integrity through newfound opportunities? Could this leap in financial gain possibly change you for the worse? Could this create you wanting more and more—where money becomes the most important pursuit for you? Might it distract you from God, your family, or your friends, focusing solely on your own significance and happiness? These are the friction and anchor points that kill many religious people's dreams.

Or do you believe that only great things will line up for your life after attaining your goal? Will achieving your goal inevitably lead you to your highest self, or to a lower self?

4. What will others think of you upon attaining this goal?

Consider this question solely framed by your Values. Will others (friends, family, neighbors, etc.) consider you uppity, greedy, selfish, materialistic, off-purpose—even it's not true? The possibility of others disliking you or criticizing you upon attaining the goal needs to be considered and evaluated. A belief that you will be disliked by those you

- YOUR WORKBOOK -
Filtering Dream Though Alpha-Values

3. What is bound to happen after you attain the goal?

Possible Objections:

4. What will others think of you upon attaining this goal?

Possible Objections:

respect will often sabotage dreams. Being liked is baked into our survival instincts. Being disliked can be considered threatening, and in our example, sabotaging your success is a tidy solution to counter this threat, especially if some external source can be blamed for our failure. Alphas, Values, and instincts will team up and keep you from that dream. However, they will also hide the evidence to keep you from feeling bad about yourself. They will restabilize the system *behind the curtains*, so to speak. They will consider it protecting you. That's their job!

At this point, hopefully your dream passed through the four Alpha-Value considerations. If so, if ALL your Alpha Beliefs approve of your dream, you may skip the next step and jump directly to STEP 4. However, if you found Alpha-Value objections to your dream, you must deal with them. You'll either need to change these limiting beliefs or change your dream. If you stick with the dream, the next step is to find the limiting Power Belief and reframe it so it works FOR you.

CHAPTER 28

STEP 3

REFRAMING OBJECTIONABLE BELIEFS

To again explain what *reframing* means and how it works, it's best to teach by example. So, let's pretend each of the considerations in the previous chapter (presented again below) uncovered an Alpha-Value objection. In other words, we discovered four Alpha-Values not in favor of you achieving your dream, which means *your highest certainty beliefs are programmed to sabotage your success!*

1. The Literal Result of Attaining $250,000?

Possible Objection: *A humble person doesn't strive for wealth in the first place.*

2. **The Intention or desire behind wanting $250,000?**

   Possible Objection: *You want success to feel important and that's egotistical.*

3. **What having $250,000 might then lead to?**

   Possible Objection: *Once you get a taste for money, you're likely to compromise yourself to keep it.*

4. **What others you care about might think of you once you have $250,000. Will they judge you as a bad character?**

   Possible Objection: *Other people will consider you materialistic and shallow for valuing money.*

One of these objections can kill your dream—all four will absolutely guarantee its failure! We need to bring your Alpha-Values in line with your dream. To do that, we need to reframe them. I'll attempt to reframe *each* objection (all four), three different ways.

We must keep with the spirit of these beliefs. No technicalities or shifty lawyering around their intent. These conclusions are trying to protect you from becoming a failed, unhappy, corrupted person.

YOUR STRATEGY: Show how the money DIRECTLY strengthens your Alpha-Values and assists you becoming your highest possible self.

POSSIBLE OBJECTION 1:

A humble person doesn't strive for wealth.

This objection gives insight into a specific character trait your belief systems feels is necessary to achieve your highest ethical and moral self. The core Value at risk is humility, modesty—being humble. Thus, when we attempt to reframe it, we need to preserve that core Value. We must strengthen it, not override it.

NOTE: These reframes will not have the same effect, certainty or results for everyone. I'm simply demonstrating by using possible conclusions for the sake of providing examples.

> **Example Reframe 1:** *Humility is not shrinking your self-worth compared with others—but rather, increasing their worth in your eyes. Being charitable to others reveals recognizing the importance of their lives. Having money helps you become more charitable.*

> **Example Reframe 2***: Money is just an amplifier. Evil people use money to become more evil. Ethical people use money to provide more justice.*

> **Example Reframe 3:** *Being humble has nothing to do with money. There are poor people who aren't humble, and there are rich people who are. It has to do with your character, not your bank balance.*

POSSIBLE OBJECTION 2:

You want success to feel important and that's egotistical.

This objection equates the feeling of importance derived from accomplishment with arrogance. It's again touching on the humility vs. arrogance motif. Reframing it, we need to present conclusions where money doesn't foster arrogance.

> **Example Reframe 1:** *A person who purposely limits their income to somehow prove they're not arrogant is just as absorbed in their self-image and self-importance as someone who doesn't limit their income.*

> **Example Reframe 2:** *Extra money doesn't make me a better human than a homeless person. It simply means I have more currency to better care for myself and others, not burdening others with having to help take care of my needs and responsibilities.*

> **Example Reframe 3:** *As a child of God, as a child of the Universe, as one of only a tiny smattering of beings that will ever experience existence, I <u>am</u> important. Feeling important is only bad if and when you then judge others' lives as not important.*

POSSIBLE OBJECTION 3:

> *Once you get a taste for money, you're likely to compromise yourself to keep it*

The spirit of this objection is not money, but the fear of compromising—getting swept away in other schemes. Doing so will prevent you from reaching your highest possible self. This belief is trying to protect you. We need to focus on the compromising aspect.

> **Example Reframe 1:** *Equating wealth with eventual corruption is an Opinion at best, a Superstition at worst. There's no universal law nor Fact requiring that wealth must eventually compromise people. There are no Facts that prove that.*

Example Reframe 2: *I'm more likely to compromise myself when I'm in financial need than when I'm in financial abundance.*

Example Reframe 3: *Succeeding at my dreams is not compromising. Purposely failing to pursue my dream is.*

POSSIBLE OBJECTION 4:

People will consider you materialistic or shallow for valuing money

This objection contains no Alpha-Values on its own, but rather plays into one's fears about the Opinions of others. Basically, it's predicting that other people will form a lower Opinion (belief) of you which will be a threat to your self-worth. Again, this objection is trying to protect you. To counter this, we need to show how money may raise people's Opinions of your character.

Example Reframe 1: *People love winners and they want to be around successful people.*

Example Reframe 2: *I value success in ALL facets of life. I value being the best me I can during this lifetime. People will see this. I don't value money—it simply rewards me for being the best me.*

Example Reframe 3: *My success can inspire so many others to go after their dreams and reach their highest potential.*

I've presented twelve possible reframes for objections discovered by filtering the dream of making $250,000 through a hypothetical Alpha-Value system. I realize most or all of those may not apply to your specific dream or your specific belief system. The examples are to help you understand the process of identifying and reframing limiting beliefs.

So now, let's give it a go with your dream. Let's walk through your Alpha-Values and see if we can find objections and solutions. You will need to pay close attention to the character and quality (what I refer to as *spirit*) of any objection you uncover. When creating a reframe, make sure you honor the Alpha-Value that is threatened. Reframe the belief so as to strengthen and protect the Alpha-Value. Learn to counter the threatening assertion brought forward in the objection with a belief of equal or higher certainty. You have many Alpha-Values that can defend your dreams. Flaunt those. Do not leave STEP 3 until you are absolutely convinced your goal serves your highest self.

- YOUR WORKBOOK -
Filtering Your Dream Though Alpha-Values

1. In what ways does attaining the literal goal put you at odds with your highest self?

Strongest Objection:

What is the spirit of the objection? What is it protecting you from?

How can achieving your dream actually deliver your highest-self more so than not achieving your dream? (Are there Alphas, Truths, Facts, and Values in your belief system that can back up this claim?)

Create three REFRAMES that support your Alpha-Values <u>and</u> the idea that accomplishing your goal will bring you closer to your highest self.

- YOUR WORKBOOK -
Filtering Dream Though Alpha-Values

2. What is the real reason you want the dream?

Strongest Objection to this reason:

What is the spirit of the objection? What negative consequences is the objection protecting you from?

Will these negative consequences prevent you from reaching your highest self? Will these negative possibilities subtract more from your destiny than accomplishing your dream will add to it?

Create three REFRAMES that support your Alpha-Values <u>and</u> the idea that accomplishing your goal will bring you closer to your highest self.

- YOUR WORKBOOK -
Filtering Dream Though Alpha-Values

3. What is bound to happen after you attain the goal?

Strongest Objection to this happening:

Is this negative outcome GUARANTEED to happen? Is this outcome a Truth or Superstition? Is it a Fact or merely a fear?

What great things could happen because you reached the goal that otherwise might not happen if you never reach it?

Create three REFRAMES that support your Alpha-Values <u>and</u> the idea that accomplishing your goal will bring you closer to your highest self.

- YOUR WORKBOOK -
Filtering Dream Though Alpha-Values

4. What will others think of you upon attaining this goal?

Strongest Condemnation of your character:

Are such thoughts by others Opinions, Facts, or Truths about your truest self?

Think of all the possible ways that achieving your dream could make you more respectable and positively influential to others. How will it help you better yourself, your family members, the world at large? Even if helps one more person live and die with a fulfilled life isn't that good for mankind?

Create three REFRAMES that support the Fact that accomplishing your dream is what your Alpha-Values want from you in this lifetime. It's what you are destined to offer the world with your life, talents, and interests.

Assert how criticisms by others toward your success points to errors in their belief system, not yours.

There is a destiny that belief fulfills.

~ Chris W. Metz

CHAPTER 29

STEP 4

FILTER YOUR DREAM THROUGH YOUR
SELF-IDENTITY BELIEFS FOR OBJECTIONS

Now that your dream has been found acceptable and reasonable to your Alpha-Values, we need to filter it through your Self-Identity beliefs to find any and all obstacles and objections that may be lurking there. Oftentimes, what's acceptable and permissible at the highest levels are still believed to be off limits to us because we feel we are personally not worthy or simply lack the abilities and talents to rise to such levels. In essence, others can become kings and queens, and even though I want to be, I'm only destined to be a pauper.

Below are four practical considerations when filtering your stated dream through your Self-Identity conclusions.

171

1. WOULD ACCOMPLISHING THIS DREAM HELP MAKE YOU A BETTER PERSON—A BETTER MOM, DAD, SON, DAUGHTER, SISTER, BROTHER, FRIEND, COLLEAGUE, NEIGHBOR, HUSBAND, OR WIFE?

Imagine in your mind you have achieved your goal. It's done. It's now written in the record book of your life. What happens now? Having accomplished this, is there any chance you're now worse off than you were before accomplishing it? Less happy? Less *you*?

At this point, let's forget the path you've had to take to accomplish the dream. Let's just focus on the fact you achieved it. Let's imagine the path was ethical and positive. (We'll deal with those other possible issues in Steps 6-9.) For now, only consider WHAT has been accomplished, not *how* it was accomplished.

In the example of earning $250,000—does having this money now make you a better person or not? Does having $250,000 make you a better mom, dad, sister, brother, friend, colleague, neighbor, husband or wife? Oftentimes there is no qualitative difference in our soul or character by simply accomplishing a goal. If my dream is to hike the Appalachian trail, or learn to play piano, lose fifty pounds, land that job promotion, or find the love of my life—afterwards, I may be stronger, smarter, healthier, wealthier—but I'm still the same person in my heart and soul. My situation may be better, but my core being is the same. That's perfectly fine. What we really need by asking this question is to discover if your subconscious mind fears this will ruin your self-identity. Accomplishing this dream cannot have you conclude you are a going to become a worse person. We can live with *I'll most likely stay the same.* What we really want is, *it will definitely make me a better person.* We cannot have—*I'll become a worse person.*

- YOUR WORKBOOK -
Filtering Dream Though Self-Identity Beliefs

1. Would accomplishing your dream make you a better person?

Possible reasons why it would not:

---

2. Would accomplishing this dream be in-line (congruent) with your perceived destiny—the life story by which you'd like to be known and remembered?

Imagine your life as a story, starting at your birth and ending at your eventual death. Is it a good story? Would someone else find it interesting? Would they sympathize and root for the main character (you)? Would accomplishing this dream make the story better or worse? Would accomplishing your dream be necessary to get the ending you truly want for your life?

If the answer is no—you may want to question your intentions for wanting to accomplish this goal. If goals don't enhance your life, make your story line better, then why put in effort and time? It's vital that your self-identity keeps pushing itself toward its perceived destiny and your highest self. Many times, we don't really know if we have a destiny or what our destiny might be? In such instances, we should follow the dreams of your heart and mind. These are clues. Follow that which inspires you. Inspiration is the magic leading you to a life story most aligned with your beliefs and desires.

- YOUR WORKBOOK -
Filtering Dream Though Self-Identity Beliefs

2. Would accomplishing this dream be in-line (congruent) with your perceived destiny—the life story by which you'd like to be known and remembered?

Possible ways in which accomplishing your dream does not represent how you'd like to be remembered:

3. Would accomplishing this be in-line (congruent) with your true personality?

This is where many people find their first objection because humans so frequently hide their truest personality and dreams from the outer world. It's a defense mechanism. It protects us from ridicule, embarrassment, or negativity. There are many people who dream of fame or some profession they believe would sound foolish or outlandish if others knew. The truth is most people dream of lives different than the one they are currently living. We all desire more fun, more excitement, more romance, more adventure, more love and recognition. For example, consider a corporate accountant whose dream is to own a charter fishing boat, taking tourists onto the ocean for a day of deep-sea fishing. Think of the secretary who wants to write novels and go on talk shows, or the pharmacist who wants to live in a cabin far from any major city, grow an organic garden and raise her family in nature. The world is filled with billions of these cross-over dreams, and the dreamers fear others will find out and consider them foolish. So, when you filter your dream through question #3, don't panic if it doesn't match up with your church and career personality. Test it against that secret personality you know is the real you. It may be uncomfortable to think you'll one day have to expose your true self in order to accomplish your dream, but you already have hundreds of internal beliefs that support your desire to confidently march forward. We just need to defuse the limiting beliefs that cause you to hide your truest personality.

- YOUR WORKBOOK -
Filtering Dream Though Self-Identity Beliefs

3. **Would accomplishing this be in-line (congruent) with your true personality?**

List any ways this dream doesn't represent the <u>truest</u> version of you:

4. Would accomplishing this dream be in-line (congruent) with your reputation?

So, what is your reputation anyway? Do you think the reputation the world has of you is the same as you have of yourself? Did you ever consider you may have two reputations; the one *you* believe, and the other the *world* believes? How would accomplishing your dream threaten either of these reputations? Would earning $250,000 enhance both reputations or diminish them? Would it convince others you're a go-getter? A winner? A success? Someone who gets things done? Or do you become a *materialist*? That person who won't stay in their lane and is a *wannabe*? It's crucial you recognize all the Self-Identity beliefs swimming around in your mind that will attempt to block your dream. Find these objections. **They are limiting you!** We'll need to examine and reframe them.

- YOUR WORKBOOK -
Filtering Dream Though Self-Identity Beliefs

4. Would accomplishing this dream be in-line (congruent) with your reputation?

List any ways accomplishing this dream would tarnish your good name or reputation:

At this point, hopefully your dream passed through all your Self-Identity filters and you can skip the reframing process and move on to STEP 6. However, **if you DID find identity objections to your dream, you must deal with them.** You'll either need to change these limiting beliefs or change your dream. And because I'm a huge advocate of pursuing your dreams, let's see if we can't simply reframe the limiting beliefs blocking your flow.

CHAPTER 30

STEP 5

REFRAMING YOUR LIMITING BELIEFS

To once again demonstrate how reframing works, let's work through some examples. Let's suppose we were able to identify four objections—one from each of the four considerations in the previous chapter which are again listed below. These objections stem from dissonance between your self-identity and realizing your goal of having $250,000.

1. Would accomplishing this dream help make you a better person—a better mom, dad, son, daughter, sister, brother, friend, colleague, neighbor, husband, or wife?

Possible Objection: *It will not make me better because I will leave my colleague-friends behind as my other career takes off.*

2. Would accomplishing this dream be in-line (congruent) with your perceived destiny—the life story by which you'd like to be known and remembered?

Possible Objection: *It seems like it would be a great high point in my story—but there's always a rise before the fall.*

3. Would accomplishing this be in-line (congruent) with your true personality?

Possible Objection: *What if my personality changes and I can't control it.*

4. Would accomplishing this be in-line (congruent) with your reputation?

Possible Objection: *I've always been a middle-class, blue-collar person. Wealth will change that.*

So those are four possible limiting beliefs we might contend with, and I'll try to reframe each three different ways.

POSSIBLE OBJECTION 1:

It will not make me a better person because I will leave my colleague-friends behind.

This is one possible way a person may see how achieving their goal of $250,000 will make them a worse person.

The reasoning could go something like this:

"The $250,000 was only a stepping stone to the million dollars I originally wanted but thought was out of range. At $250,000 I will have assets and new contacts that make reaching a million a more realistic possibility. However, to go after the higher amount I will move further and further away from the longtime friendships I've formed at my current job. I will in effect literally leave good people and friends behind for the pursuit of more money."

What becomes obvious here is that loyalty and friendship are high values associated with the person's identity. People are more important than money. If they "move on" to pursue greater opportunities, they have become disloyal and snooty to their friends simply because they put money before friendship. Therefore, all our reframes need to preserve these revealed Values. Explain how your eventual success will strengthen your relationships.

> **Example Reframe 1:** *I won't be leaving them behind; I'm going to prove to them we all can go after our dreams. At that point, I'll have the credibility to teach them how Power Beliefs may be blocking them from their goals.*

> **Example Reframe 2:** *Having more money and connections will allow me to help my colleague-friends in ways I currently cannot.*

> **Example Reframe 3:** *They're not going to think I abandoned them. They're loyal to me, also. They'll be happy for me. More likely than not they'll tease me about having to pick up the check when we all go out.*

POSSIBLE OBJECTION 2:

It seems like it would be a great high point in my story —but there's always a rise before the fall.

For many people, success delivers a new pressure—the pressure of keeping it. In religious fables or the archetypal stories passed down through history, there are many cautionary tales about flying too high. We have all heard modern tales of someone who couldn't handle some blessing that came into their life and they ended up ruining it. For instance, the lottery winner who loses millions and ends up broke, or the unassuming guy who lands the dream girl, only to drive her away by his insecurities and jealousy, or the on-the-rise politician who gets caught in some scandal. We've been taught that rising above one's station is fraught with possible disaster.

I was recently discussing life with a childhood friend and was telling her how happy I was. How I've arrived at a place in my life where everything was going great. She replied something to the effect of, *if that were me, I would now be worried something bad was going to happen.* She obviously has a belief that success and doom must run together, each cycling one after the other so as to never truly let peace and happiness take root. I'm unsure where her belief came from. Direct experience? Pattern recognition? Emotion? And I'm unsure what category she assigned it. Superstition? Fact? Alpha? If this may be something you also conclude, we should learn to counter it.

So how do we reframe beliefs of the *rise-before-the-fall* variety? It may be helpful to find popular storylines that resonate with you. Plots wherein we enjoy the story more because the hero/heroine took the risk—they went after their dream and won. Sports movies are ripe with these examples. All rags to riches stories, adventures, and pop love stories have the characters winning in the end.

Example Reframe 1: *Is a belief that a rise must always result in a fall a Truth, a Fact, an Opinion, or Superstition? You could say that Cinderella rose at the ball, fell at midnight, but then ultimately rose again to marry the Prince. Or, you might say Ebenezer Scrooge's monetary success lead to his eventual fall—but it didn't. The ghosts helped improve his character even more. His life got even better.*

Example Reframe 2: *A rise before the fall is only in tragic storylines. I've decided to rewrite my story. From here going forward, my life is an action-adventure, romantic comedy. It's my life and dictated primarily through my beliefs. I now believe rise and fall stories are sad and cliché. I'm not a character in one of those.*

Example Reframe 3: *The fall that happens in tragic dramas isn't because of 250,000 literal dollars attached to my net worth, but rather because a latent character flaw appears and turns me bad. It's not the money, it's something already in your personality you'll have to deal with. See previous reframes for Objection 1 (the goal makes you a worse person) to reassure yourself against this, or see reframes from Objection 3 and 4 listed below.*

POSSIBLE OBJECTION 3:

What if my personality changes and I can't stop it?

The fear here, regarding self-identity, has two components: 1) the person will change, and 2) they won't be able to control the change. The person believes their life will somehow be outside their control. This is a major threat to the mind's addiction for stability and certainty. To reframe such a belief, we need to explain how change can provide greater certainty and stability to the personality.

> **Example Reframe 1:** *In order to achieve my dream, my personality does not need to change. However, my knowledge and habits will change. I will most likely have to become more disciplined, able to handle more stress and solve more problems. This helps me stabilize other areas of my life. If it was easy to have $250,000, everyone would have it. The abilities I gain through achieving my goal will make me a better person; MORE capable of controlling my thoughts and actions, not less.* **New Belief:** *$250,000 will change me for the better while giving me more control over my beliefs and behaviors.*

> **Example Reframe 2:** *My personality* **must** *change. I welcome this as I am nowhere near living as my highest self.*

> **Example Reframe 3:** *Is an out-of-control personality change rooted more in Superstition or Fact? How certain am I that 1) my personality will change for the worse, and 2) I won't be able to stop it? Worry is always based on not being able to predict the outcome. Worry is always based on low certainty beliefs.*

POSSIBLE OBJECTION 4:

I've always been a middle-class, blue-collar person. Wealth will change that.

This objection is really conveying at an identity level that being blue collar and middle class is the best one can be. Anything outside blue collar must be bad. To reframe, you either redefine middle class, or imbue upper socioeconomic levels as having good people as well.

> **Example Reframe 1:** *The labels blue collar and middle class describe one's job category and how much money one makes per year—not how good of a person one is.*

> **Example Reframe 2:** *On my tombstone, I'd rather have them engrave "Lived a happy, fulfilled life" than simply "Blue collar and Middle class." If I'm given one life to live, I'm going to strive for my dream, not generic labels impressed upon me by Authority Downloads.*

> **Example Reframe 3:** *Blue collar, middle class people are admirable, not because they lack money, but because they have decent Values and work ethic. I have blue collar, middle class Values and work ethic. But I can do without the low wages! Nobody wants low wages! Ask any blue collar person you come across.*

So, there we go. Those are three possible reframes per identity objection to help you overcome objections that threaten to sabotage your dream. Tailor your reframes to the specific objections (if any) and to your specific belief system. At this point if everything's in favor of the $250,000 goal, you are now ready to test the second half of your dream—the **Action Plan**. The Action Plan includes the behavior and activities needed to accomplish the dream in the first place. After completing your workbook, particular to your specific dream and belief system, you can move on to STEP 6.

- YOUR WORKBOOK -
Filtering Dream Though Self-Identity Beliefs

1. **Would accomplishing this dream help make you a better person—a better mom, dad, son, daughter, sister, brother, friend, colleague, neighbor, husband, or wife?**

Most convincing way it would NOT make you a better person:

What Values would be lost along the way in order for your dream to have made you a worse person? To accomplish your dream was losing those Values an absolute must?

Think of all the possible ways that achieving your dream could make you a better person. Ways that might not be available to you if you didn't achieve it.

Create three REFRAMES that support the Fact that accomplishing your dream is critical to maximizing your potential and making you the best person, mom, dad, son, daughter, sister, brother, friend, colleague, citizen, neighbor, wife or husband. Do not use Hope or Opinion beliefs in arguing this case. Use Values, Facts, and Truths.

- YOUR WORKBOOK -
Filtering Dream Though Self-Identity Beliefs

2. **Would accomplishing this dream be congruent with your perceived destiny—the life story by which you'd like to be known and remembered?**

Most powerful way in which it strays from your destiny:

Do you fear a "rise before the fall" outcome? Do you fear that once you have accomplished your dream you may have to pay for it with unpleasant costs delivered by fate? Are such beliefs Superstitions? What's the level of certainty do you have that reality is truly built like this?

Focus on the clues and signals you've received over your lifetime that you are destined to do something meaningful with your talents and interests. Remember—on your deathbed it will not be the things you've done that you most regret, but rather the things you didn't do. The things you didn't try or pursue because of fear or other excuses.

Create three REFRAMES that support the Fact that accomplishing your dream is a necessary part of your destiny. Argue with Values, Facts, and Truths that your life journey won't be as meaningful or as satisfying should you give up on your dream.

- YOUR WORKBOOK -
Filtering Dream Though Self-Identity Beliefs

3. Would accomplishing your dream be congruent with your true personality?

How is the dream in conflict with your truest self?

If I could know your soul, would it make sense to me that you should have this dream and desire it for your life's story? Does the dream reveal anything about you that you've hidden from the world? Did faulty beliefs (Opinions, Superstitions) cause you to hide it from the world?

Think of all the possible ways that achieving your dream could free you to become the person you've always wanted to be.

Create three REFRAMES that support the Fact that accomplishing your dream is necessary for you to become the person you were truly born to be. Explain how achieving your dream is the only way your truest personality can manifest and shine.

- YOUR WORKBOOK -
Filtering Dream Though Self-Identity Beliefs

4. Would accomplishing your dream be in-line with your reputation?

Strongest way your dream could lessen your reputation:

Should one's reputation be built on accomplishments or failures? Should it be motivated by an inner calling or the Opinions of others?

You've already determined your dream will make you a better person, moving you closer to your highest self...how does it not enhance your reputation? What Values can possibly get corrupted, and how can you ensure they don't?

Create three REFRAMES that support the Fact that accomplishing your dream is the reputation you were born for. It's what you are destined to offer the world with your talents and interests.

Beliefs are so powerful because they
dictate our efforts and actions.

~ Shawn Achor

CHAPTER 31

STEP 6

FILTER YOUR ACTION PLAN THROUGH YOUR ALPHA-VALUES

D o the ends justify the means? All dreams require some form of action, activity, and behavior. In order to achieve any dream you'll have to perform some series of behaviors that will move you closer to your dream, introduce you to new people, and most likely cause you to go outside your comfort zone. Currently your mind has, at the very least, Hopes and Opinions about HOW you will achieve your dream and what you will have to do to get there. If the actions necessary to achieve your dream threaten Power Beliefs in your **Alpha-Values** or **self-identity,** you will once again create friction and opposition.

In our $250,000 goal example, let's pretend the $55,000 per year teacher wants to start an online business to accomplish her goal. At this stage, it doesn't really matter what she does as long as it doesn't violate her Alpha-Values.

So here are some valuable considerations:

> *Are these **behaviors** illegal or will they in any way destroy another person's life, liberty, property, or malign their good reputation?*
>
> *Do you consider the **behaviors** shameful or indecent?*
>
> *Besides delivering your dream, will these **behaviors** help other sentient life or the environment along the way?*

Like we did before with your goals, determine if you have any single Power Belief pushing back against you executing the behaviors needed to accomplish the $250,000 goal. If so, you'll need to reframe them keeping the spirit of the Alpha-Values intact.

It's much more difficult reframing beliefs about behaviors. Actions have a reality altogether different than thoughts and ideas which merely live in your own head. Behaviors enter external reality and have effects that can be experienced by others. Behaviors that violate one's Alpha-Values will undoubtedly deal blows to one's self-identity, self-respect, and self-esteem. Many soldiers are haunted by the behaviors they had to carry out that violated their Alpha-Values.

If you find objections to your Action Plan when passing them through the three considerations listed above, my recommendation is to find a way to **change your game plan**, not reframe your Alpha-Values. We do not need to destabilize your entire belief system with actions that cannot be undone. We simply need to find a different way to earn $250,000 that is acceptable to your highest beliefs.

There are many pathways that can lead you to your dreams. Your highest self is waiting to be realized. Never give up. Find the **best** route. The one that not only gets you there, but deeply resonates with your belief system. That path, that course, that action plan is a like a giant sail. When you find it, your subconscious mind will become the gales that carry you to your destination.

Beliefs are the determinants of what one experiences.
There are no external 'causes.'

~ David R. Hawkins

CHAPTER 32

STEP 7

FILTER YOUR ACTION PLAN THROUGH YOUR SELF-IDENTITY BELIEFS

I would like to share a final story with you to illustrate the power of self-identity, and how your own may get in the way. It dates back to that dark period of my life referenced earlier. I was severely underemployed and could barely make ends meet. There were days I literally had $10 in my bank account. I had three small children and I did a lot of soul searching as to how I could make more money and what I'd be willing to do. I remember a strange idea popping into my head. I knew a person who was a salesman—a peddler, hustling jewelry, cooking knives at stores, etc. He pretty much felt comfortable selling anything to anybody, anywhere. I questioned whether I would be willing to do that. What would I be willing to sell and what wouldn't I? A scenario popped into my mind: a crazy notion of selling wristwatches off my arm in the parking lot of a county fair as people walked by. I had encountered salesmen trying to hawk watches and handbags on street corners before, but could I do that? To make money (which I desperately needed), was I willing to solicit strangers to buy wrist-watches? The answer that came back to me was even more strange. For some reason, I would not allow myself to hawk watches and earn money to benefit me and my family, but (and this is the strange part) I would be willing to do so to raise money for some charity I believed in. *WHAT?!* Yes, I was willing to sell watches to strangers—but only if it didn't benefit me? That is a factual discovery about myself.

Probing this incongruity further, it dawned on me that my self-identity, self-worth, and self-respect (which was already at its lowest point) considered selling watches in parking lots as a shady, unprofessional hustle. That was, of course, just my Opinion. Even though it could have put money in my pocket and food in my kids mouths, I believed it to be a hustle, not a legitimate way to make a living. I somehow deemed it *beneath* me. And yet at the same time my identity found it permissible to hawk watches if it was in the name of a greater cause from which I had no financial gain. What a startling lesson in the programming of our beliefs! Contrary to what the world tells us:

We do NOT act in our own best interests.
We act in accordance with our own self-identity.

Your self-identity is like an onion, with layers and layers of nuances forming the whole. There are actions that are just unacceptable for you to imagine doing for X—but acceptable for Y. The good news is most of your self-identity objections are based in fears at the **Superstition** and **Opinion** levels, and you should be able to deal with them effectively through reframes with a little practice.

Below is a list of limiting, yet popular identity beliefs that may get in the way once you filter your Action Plan through your self-identity filter:

I'm not smart enough

I don't have the experience

I'm too old/too young

I wouldn't know how to do that

I'm not good with people

I hate selling

I don't understand business

I don't understand (fill in the blank)

I have the wrong background

I'm damaged goods

I'm unlovable

I panic under pressure

I won't fit in

I wish I had a quick and easy way to reframe all limiting self-identity beliefs because these are the dominant issues most people battle. As you have learned, there are many ways such beliefs came about, and without understanding what birthed these Power Beliefs, and which categories house them, it's hard to switch all of them off with a single reframe.

The important thing to do is dissect the most powerful one for its level of certainty. For example, let's say there's a very high certainty in the belief, *I hate selling.* If the certainty is at the *Values* category or above, ask yourself if you'd be willing to work on and improve this flaw IF it would guarantee you your dreams? So, if you hate the idea of selling, would you be willing to work on that? If you don't understand business, would you be willing to take classes or find a mentor? If you panic under pressure, would you be willing to find a coach or therapist to help you manage this?

If the answer is NO

Congratulations!—you just found one badass limiting Power Belief blocking you from everything you want. That is the prize! That is what this book has been trying to help you discover. Eureka! You found it.

An identity-belief that refuses to waver in order to deliver your dream is a Power Belief that may need outside, professional attention to unblock. Don't feel like you have to eliminate it on you own. This is your dream. Your destiny. Fight for it.

If the answer is YES

One way to start is to mentally cluster previous actions and behaviors that *disprove the certainty* of the limiting belief. For instance, if the limiting belief is *I hate selling,* consider all the times you have tried selling people on things outside of actual financial transactions. Have you ever tried to convince a friend they should or shouldn't date a particular person? That is selling. Have you ever tried to persuade someone they should try a restaurant or watch a great Netflix special? Those are also forms of selling—they just don't involve a product/service and payment. Sales is simply influencing another to do something they will enjoy or will improve their life. Recognizing the best aspects of selling helps reframe the meaning of sales which will reduce the certainty in the belief *I hate selling*. If someone asked if they could buy your broom and dustpan for $100, would you refuse and tell them you hate selling?

Doing these mental exercises will start to clarify your original limiting Power Belief (*I hate selling*), and you will eventually discover the specific aspect of selling you are truly opposed to. Let's pretend after some deliberation you discover your actual objection to selling is *I do not want to sell something people don't want*. Well, there's a belief we can embrace to your advantage. If you need to sell products or services to make the $250,000, just make sure it's something people actually want, and never pressure anyone who doesn't seem to want it. Let your identity and Alpha-Values work *for* your goals and dreams. Let them be the wind that pushes you forward.

FINAL ADVICE

Remember—this is your only life. You are currently separated from your dreams by a mere sequence of activities. Between you and your destiny is literally a sequence of behaviors, actions, and events that need only occur for you to live the life of your dreams. Executing those actions is all that stands between this minute and the person you've dreamed of being. Consider that. Those actions are all that separates you from greatness, from having the things you desire, from bettering the world by having one less human sorrowful with regret or dissatisfaction.

Your belief system controls you. For better or worse, it is the programming that determines what you will do, what you'll attempt, and what you'll risk. But it is merely programming. It is there to serve your life, not encumber it. You may be one belief away...or you may be ten beliefs away. But the fact is, the only thing stopping you— is figuring out **how to overcome your resistance** toward executing those behaviors and actions that delivers your dreams.

As one of the few beings that ever gets to experience the magic of being alive, you play a significant role in the unfolding story of humanity. Currently, you may believe you have little impact on the world and its trajectory. And at this moment, perhaps that's an actual Fact. But achieve your dreams and you'll discover *your story* offers inspiration and fire to those who hear about it. Seven billion people want to believe their dreams can come true. You can help light the path for them to succeed. Your success can inspire a dozen others, who inspire hundreds, who possibly inspire millions. You *are* significant.

So here is my final request: **Stay Inspired. The world depends upon it.**

BELIEF ASSESSMENT REDO

Having reached the end of the book, I have high certainty you can now identify a belief from a mile away. You just need to ask yourself, *is this a conclusion?* I also have confidence you can match your beliefs to the appropriate category in which you've assigned them. It may take some thoughtful analysis, but you'll eventually discover the level of certainty you have in any belief that's programmed into your mind.

Having already told you 38 of the 40 items presented below are beliefs, can you now confidently determine which two are not beliefs?

WHICH TWO ARE NOT BELIEFS?

1. _____ Possums are reptiles

2. _____ I think I'll go workout after dinner

3. _____ It's impossible for minorities to be racist

4. _____ It's raining outside

5. _____ The sun rises in the east and sets in the west

6. _____ I assume the cop had on a bullet proof vest

7. _____ Triangles have 3 sides

8. _____ If you work hard, success is guaranteed

9. _____ I hate reading

10. _____ *"Dr. Livingston, I presume."*

11. _____ A tree has more consciousness than grass

12. _____ White owls are evil

13. _____ The sun is a nearly perfect sphere of hot plasma at the center of our solar system

14. _____ 2+2=4

15. _____ My favorite food is pizza

16. _____ I love my children

17. _____ There is either a God, or there is not. There is no other possibility.

18. _____ The speed of light is roughly 186,000 miles/second

19. _____ Area 51 is where they hide the UFO's

20. _____ Oswald killed Kennedy using karate

21. _____ Oswald didn't kill Kennedy

22. _____ For better or for worse, in sickness and in health

23. _____ Abe Lincoln was the 16th President of the U.S.

24. _____ Women are physically weaker than men

25. _____ I think, therefore I am

26. _____ That guy looks like my Uncle Tony

27. _____ My wife snores every night

28. _____ January 1st begins a new calendar year

29. _____ All Camrys are cars, but not all cars are Camrys

30. _____ Men are mortal

31. _____ Chicken soup restores health

32. _____ Columbus, Ohio is similar to Atlanta, Georgia

33. _____ We are born with ten fingers and ten toes

34. _____ I feel that nobody knows the truth

35. _____ Would you rather be rich or happy

36. _____ Becky Lustanza got nailed for copyright violation

37. _____ I have a hunch she's not coming to the wedding

38. _____ A foolish consistency is the hobgoblin of little minds

39. _____ There are only 2 cookies left in the cookie jar

40. _____ Wow, your son has really grown over the summer

The following two items are not beliefs.

#_____ and #_____

Note: You'll find the answer to which items are not beliefs on page 103 below the quote...or simply review questions twenty-two and thirty-five. The first does not assert any conclusion as written, and the second is a question, not a conclusion.

Printed in Great Britain
by Amazon

17450660R00127